Battlecruiser Invincible
The history of the
first battlecruiser, 1909–16

Battlecruiser
Invincible
The history of the
first battlecruiser, 1909–16

V. E. Tarrant

NAVAL INSTITUTE PRESS

To three little ladies
Val
Tinker and Tabatha
who make it all worthwhile

First published in Great Britain
in 1986 by Arms and Armour Press Limited,
2–6 Hampstead High Street, London NW3 1QQ.

**Published and distributed in the United States of America
by the Naval Institute Press, Annapolis, Maryland 21402**

Library of Congress Catalog Card No. 86 63434

ISBN: 0-87021-147-1

This edition is authorised for sale only in the United States
and its territories and possessions

The illustrations in this book have been collected
from many sources, and vary in quality owing to the variety
of circumstances under which they were taken and preserved.
As a result, certain of the illustrations are not of the
standard to be expected from the best of today's equipment,
materials and techniques. They are nevertheless included
for their inherent information value, to provide an
authentic visual coverage of the subject.

Designed by David Gibbons; edited by Michael Boxall;
typeset by Typesetters (Birmingham) Ltd., camerawork by
Anglia Repro Ltd., Rayleigh; printed and bound in
Great Britain by Billing and Sons Ltd.

Contents

List of Maps

Foreword
by Captain C. H. Layman,
DSO, LVO, RN

HMS *Invincible*
at sea

Ship's names are poetic words, deeply laden with associations. And of all the ship's names in the annals of the Royal Navy, *Invincible* must be one of the most evocative. It is a splendidly arrogant name, seeming to challenge fate and defy the consequences.

The first ship to bear the name was built as the French 74 *L'Invincible*, captured by Admiral Anson in 1747, commissioned as HMS *Invincible*, and sunk in 1758 on the Horse Tail Bank; she is now being carefully salvaged by a small team of enthusiasts from the Portsmouth Sub Aqua Club. The present *Invincible*, which is the sixth of the name and which I have the privilege to command, was commissioned in 1980 in the presence of Her Majesty the Queen and played a part in the Falklands campaign of 1982. At that time I was in a frigate in the inshore waters of the islands, and we were greatly reassured by her presence not far away. The subject of this book, *Invincible* the fifth, had an amazingly busy and varied life from 1909 to 1916, being the flagship of another Falklands campaign in 1914, before being blown up at Jutland eighteen months later, with fearful loss of life.

From the bridge of *Indomitable* my grandfather watched her explode, perplexed by the speed of her destruction and astonished at the immense column of black smoke. Many years later he described that shattering scene to me. A small fragment from *Invincible* had landed at his feet, and he picked it up and kept it. After the war he had it mounted in a gold brooch for my grandmother to wear as a reminder of a fine ship and a famous occasion. My wife, for the same reasons, now wears it when she comes on board.

7

The battlecruiser *Invincible*, as the first of her new and powerful class, was well known both inside and outside the Service throughout her life, and it is her story which the author has pieced together so well, using many hitherto unpublished sources. It makes absorbing reading, a fascinating insight into the naval life of that remarkable age with its hopes and fears, problems and successes, in peace and war. As always luck and bad luck played a part; warfare is a risk-taking business. It is easy to see now that mistakes were made in ship design and sometimes tactical manoeuvring, but I think we should not be too surprised or dismayed about that, because historians will always have the advantage over naval architects and naval tacticians.

It is obvious from these unpublished sources that, despite the momentous events which were happening around them, the men who confided their everyday thoughts to letters and journals led lives in many ways very similar to our own. Most aspects of naval life that they describe seem entirely familiar today: boats still get into difficulties, collisions happen in thick fog, and ratings chalk rude messages to the enemy on bombs and shells. It is the continuity of experience, as well as the continuity of name, which makes one feel part of a distinguished tradition. This book does well to record it.

C. H. LAYMAN
Captain

Preface

At 6.34 p.m. on 31 May 1916, the battlecruiser HMS *Invincible*, while in action during the battle of Jutland, was rent apart by a colossal magazine explosion. Earlier in the battle two other battlecruisers, *Indefatigable* and *Queen Mary*, were lost in exactly the same manner, causing Vice-Admiral Beatty to make his famous remark: 'There seems to be something wrong with our bloody ships today.'

What was wrong? Jellicoe and the senior officers of the fleet, including Beatty, were in no doubt that the three battlecruisers were lost primarily because of 'the indifferent armour protection . . . particularly as regards turret armour and deck plating'. (*Jellicoe's Jutland Despatch*). My theme, like Ariadne's thread, running through the distinguished operational history of *Invincible*, is to show conclusively that the fatal weakness was without doubt the insufficient scale of armour protection, especially with regard to the deck plating which was inadequate to protect the magazine from plunging shells fired at long range. Despite the consensus between the senior officers at sea and the Lords of the Admiralty on this point, it was argued by some, notably the Director of Naval Construction, Eustace Tennyson-d'Eyncourt, that *Invincible* and the other battlecruisers were not lost through shells penetrating the protective decks and 'Exploding either in the magazines or so close to it as to ignite the Contents' (*DNC memo of 19 December 1916. PRO ADM 86/628*). He maintained that the major culprit was *flash*, caused by a shell *penetrating the turret armour* [my italics] and bursting, resulting in the ignition of the Cordite Charges in the turret which sent a flash of high velocity flame down the 60-foot hoist into the handing room and thence into the magazine. But even Professor Marder, who goes to considerable lengths to castigate 'the legend of the battlecruisers' indifferent armour protection', has to admit that the DNC's argument was a contradiction in terms in that *'had a battlecruiser's turret not been penetrated* (because of the insufficient armour), *the . . .* (flash) *. . . would not have mattered and there would not have been any explosions'*. (see A. J. Marder: *From The Dreadnought To Scapa Flow*, vol III, p. 267, OUP, 1978).

That the DNC, who was officially responsible for the design of the battlecruisers, should mount arguments against the penetration theory and Beatty's assertion that 'our methods of ship construction are seriously at fault', is perhaps understandable, but hardly impartial, wedded as he was to his technical conviction that the fundamental maxim of British Warship design was 'the best defence is superior power of offence'. In practice, as in the case of *Invincible* and all twelve subsequent battlecruisers built for the Royal Navy, this amounted to reducing the scale of affordable armour plate to its lowest limit so that the saving in weight could ensure high speed and the carrying of the heaviest calibre of naval ordnance.

Tragedy was to be the final proof of the fallaciousness of this maxim. The design of *Hood*, the last battlecruiser built for the Royal Navy, ironically enough laid down on the very day that *Invincible*, the first battlecruiser, was destroyed, was altered to embody the lessons of Jutland. Although numerous complex measures were built in to ensure the inviolability of the magazines from flash, the greater part of the additional 5,000 tons of armour, decided necessary, was worked into the hull, leaving her slightly improved deck armour as woefully inadequate against plunging shells as that of *Invincible*. And so it came about, on that fatal morning of 24 May 1941, almost 25 years to the day on which *Invincible* blew up, a 15-inch shell fired by the German battleship *Bismarck* penetrated *Hood*'s thin deck armour and exploded in or near her after magazines, causing the ship to blow up in exactly the same manner as the three battlecruisers at Jutland.

With those four proud ships, a total of 4,722 officers and men paid with their lives, primarily, I suspect, because the judgement of successive naval designers and constructors was unduly influenced by the haunting but meaningless phrases of *Invincible*'s creator, Lord Fisher, who believed that 'speed is the best protection', and 'hitting is the thing, not armour'.

V. E. Tarrant
Cardiff.
January, 1986.

Acknowledgements

I wish to express my sincere thanks to the following for answering my inquiries and their kind permission to quote from the copyright material indicated:

The 6th Viscount Hood, from the papers of his father, Rear-Admiral Sir Horace Lambert Alexander Hood; Captain R. R. Stewart, RN, from his wartime diary and photographs from his private collection; Captain H. H. Dannreuther, RN, for providing a photograph of his father, the late Rear-Admiral H. E. Dannreuther; Mrs G. M. Schofield from the papers of her late husband, Vice-Admiral B. B. Schofield; Mrs Grace Duckworth, from the papers of her late husband, Captain Arthur Dyce Duckworth, RN, and providing photographs; Mrs C. M. McEwan from the diary of her late husband, Lieutenant-Commander Alan McEwan, RN, and providing photographs; Mrs E. Y. Allan, from the papers of her late father, Commander C. F. Laborde, RN; the Trustees of the National Maritime Museum, from the diary of Assistant Paymaster Clement Woodland, RNR; Commander T. G. P. Crick for reading the typescript and his constructive comments; Mr Bryan Gasson, the only living member of the six survivors of the loss of *Invincible* at Jutland, for his stimulating conversation and vivid recollections of his remarkable escape from the fiery clutches of death which claimed the lives of 1,021 of his shipmates; my grandmother for her recollections concerning her brother, Able Seaman George Pym, who perished with the ship. Thanks also to the staffs of the following institutions for their kind assistance: The Imperial War Museum; The Public Record Office, Kew; The National Maritime Museum; The Naval Historical Library, Ministry of Defence; and the Reference Department of Cardiff Central Library. Finally, heartfelt thanks to my brother for his sterling efforts in typing the manuscript in record time.

The following publishers have kindly given their permission to quote extracts from published works: The Navy Records Society: E. W. R. Lumby's *Papers Relating to Naval Policy and Operations in the Mediterranean 1911–1915*. John Murray Ltd: Commander

The Hon. Barry Bingham's *Falklands, Jutland and the Bight*. William Blackwood and Sons: Four Articles by Paymaster Gordon Franklyn, which appeared in various 1916 issues of Blackwood's Magazine. Macmillan Ltd: Fawcett and Hooper's *The Fighting at Jutland*. Clarendon Press, Oxford: *Dictionary of National Biography*. Curtis Brown Ltd: Richard Hough's *The Pursuit of Admiral von Spee*. Unpublished Crown Copyright material (Admiralty and Cabinet office papers) is published by permission of the Controller of Her Majesty's Stationery Office.

I have been unable to trace the copyright holders of the following and apologise for any inadvertent infringement of copyright: Letter from 'Fred' in the papers of Major W. F. Vernon; the privately published edition of Alexander Scrimgeour's Journals and Letters; the diary of ship's Corporal, Marine Albert Lee. All these papers are deposited in the archives of the Imperial War Museum. An article by Able Seaman Earnest Dandridge entitled 'The Price of Victory' which was published in a 1916 edition of *The London Magazine*.

V.E.T.

1

Fisher's Brainchild
A Super Cruiser

Throughout the latter part of the nineteenth century and the first decade of the twentieth, the British Admiralty was haunted by the nightmare spectre of *la guerre de course*: the avowed policy of France, Russia and Germany to attack British seaborne trade with swarms of marauding cruisers in the event of war. The submarine, still in its infancy, was not yet, because of its very limited range of action, considered to be a menace. As two-thirds of Britain's principal foodstuffs were being imported from overseas, she would be very quickly starved into submission unless her mercantile fleet could be adequately protected.

Before the turn of the century, it was considered that the strategic, though far from infallible, solution was for British cruisers, singly or in squadrons, to patrol up and down the terminal or focal areas of trade, which would be the obvious hunting-grounds of enemy cruisers. But when Intelligence reports indicated that the Germans had made preparations to arm a large number of their transatlantic liners to act as auxiliary cruisers, the problem had to be re-evaluated. These great ocean-going ships had speed and, more essentially, coal storage capacities so great that they could outrun and outstay any existing British cruiser. The logical answer which first presented itself was to arm Britain's own fast ocean-going liners, especially the new 25-knot Cunarders (*Lusitania* and *Mauretania*) which would be a match for the German liners. But, Fisher, the First Sea Lord, argued that 'such vessels when armed would only be equal to the German vessels', and his flamboyant dictum was that 'in war equality would not suffice'. In true Nelsonian tradition, he wanted the Royal Navy to be 100 per cent stronger than the enemy.

To ensure the inviolacy of the maritime trade routes Fisher planned to have a cruiser capable of dogging, hunting down, and destroying any enemy cruiser; the dogging to continue, if necessary, to the world's end. He set about the drawing up of a super-cruiser of revolutionary design, so large, fast, and powerfully gunned, that she could 'overtake and gobble up, like an armadillo let loose on an anthill, any enemy cruisers foolish enough to wander about British trade routes'. Five sketch designs for the proposed super-cruiser, which he named *Invincible*, were prepared and submitted to a special committee of design consisting of seven naval and seven civilian experts under the chairmanship of Fisher himself.

Having decided upon the main desiderata of size, type of propulsion and ordnance, the final drawings, prepared by the naval constructors' department, were completed by June 1905. The tender to build the ship was won by Armstrong, Whitworth & Company, and they laid down the keel at their Elswick yard, Tyneside on 2 April 1906.

In comparison to all existing cruisers they were giving birth to a monster. *Invincible*'s displacement of 17,250 tons would make her 8,200 tons heavier than the most powerful German cruiser, *Roon*, and her overall length of 567 feet would make her the longest warship in the world (148 feet longer than *Roon* and 40 feet longer than the largest British battleship – *Dreadnought*).

Four Parsons turbines, and thirty-one Yarrow boilers, generating 41,000shp, gave her a designed speed of 25 knots; two knots faster than any German liner, five knots faster than *Roon* and seven knots faster than any battleship built or building for the German navy.

But it was her offensive power that would bestow the ultimate accolade, to make her – after *Dreadnought* – the most powerful warship in existence. *Invincible* was to carry eight of the mightiest pieces of naval ordnance yet developed – the 58-ton, 45 calibre, 12-inch gun Mark X. Each gun, paired in four turrets, could throw an 850lb shell to a distance of eight and a half miles. With a firing rate of two rounds per gun per minute, this meant she could hurl 4½ tons of high explosive shell every sixty seconds, which would spell devastation to any enemy cruiser unlucky enough to fall foul of her. As the midship wing turrets were sited *en echelon*, only six of the eight guns could be brought to bear for a broadside, but this weight of shell alone was 5,100 pounds in a single salvo, almost ten times heavier than the broadside of any German cruiser and four times as great as any existing German battleship. Well could she bear the name *Invincible*.

On the overcast afternoon of Saturday, 13 April 1907, just over a year after the laying down of the keel, *Invincible* was launched by Lady Allendale. The launching was described in the *Newcastle Weekly Chronicle*. 'The ceremony was performed by Lady Allendale in the presence of thousands of people. The management had a number of stands erected almost the whole length of the vessel, and from these an excellent view of the proportions of the new cruiser was obtained. The stands were crowded by a gay company of ladies and gentlemen, while hundreds of people crowded every portion of the yard that favoured a view of the new warship. At three o'clock, Lady Allendale broke a bottle of champagne encased in flowers over the bows of the vessel which glided gracefully into the water, without the slightest hitch. As the *Invincible* was moving down the ways to the accompaniment of great cheering, a band played "Rule Britannia", followed by the national anthem.'

Invincible's subsequent fitting out on the Tyne was dogged with labour disputes, which delayed her completion by three months. Matters weren't helped when, on 28 December 1907, the collier *Oden* collided with the ship, stoving in five bottom plates and buckling beams and frames in the hull.

During the first week of March 1909, when *Invincible* was nearing completion, she left her moorings in the Tyne to undergo gunnery exercises in the Cromarty Firth. The trials were not without their lighter side as Captain Mark Kerr, who had been appointed to command the ship on 8 September 1908, relates: 'Early morning in the Cromarty Firth was calm, but later the sea became extremely rough for working the targets, and so, taking the officers, quartermasters, and sergeants of marines into my confidence, we had the clock put on ten minutes every hour until we had got a start of two hours on the sun. The men were getting up at 3.30 in the morning, and we got through all our gunnery work before the sea got too high. I remember hearing some men, smoking after their supper in the evening, remarking that they knew that daylight continued much longer in Scotland than in England, but they never knew that they would be "turning in" at ten o'clock with the sun still high in the sky. When the gunnery practices were over at the end of the week we returned to harbour, and not until the liberty men landed in the 3.30 p.m. boat and found that it was only 1.30 p.m. on shore, did they realise the pious fraud that had been played on them.'

Officially completed on 16 March 1909, she sailed from her birthplace on the Tyne during the afternoon of 18 March, under Kerr's command, bound for Portsmouth, where she was to join the Home Fleet. The journey south was not without incident, for during the dark hours of the following morning, with Great Yarmouth some miles off *Invincible*'s starboard bow, she collided with the brigantine *Mary Ann*. With her wooden bows shattered, the *Mary Ann* was in danger of floundering, and *Invincible* had to stand by her until the lifeboat *John Burch*, which had been launched from Yarmouth in response to the firing of a distress gun, took her in tow. Arriving in Portsmouth harbour on 20 March, *Invincible* secured alongside the South Railway jetty and was formally commissioned by Captain Kerr into the Royal Navy, for service in the 1st Cruiser Squadron.

Fisher was delighted with his creation, calling her a 'greyhound of the sea', and a 'New Testament ship', boasting that *Invincible* had rendered all other cruisers useless, and that no number or combination of conventional cruisers would be of the slightest avail against this armadillo of the seas. With her long, sleek hull, ram bow, sturdy tripod masts, three funnels, and huge menacing guns, she did appear to be the very summation of sea power: long, lean, ferociously handsome: the unchallengeable guardian of the trade routes. But all was not quite as well as it seemed.

18

2

Portents of Doom
The Fatal Flaw

Invincible was not, of course, to be the sole guardian of Britain's huge mercantile fleet of some 10,000,000 tons. In the naval estimates for 1905–06 a further three ships of the *Invincible* class were allowed for, one being dropped before the tenders were contracted out. Two sister ships were laid down in 1906: the *Inflexible* at John Brown's yard, Clydebank and the *Indomitable* by Fairfield at the Seven Yard, Govan. Fisher then ordered another three of these large armoured cruisers (as they were originally classified) under the 1908 estimates, which he boasted 'would make the Germans gnash their teeth'. These were the ships of the *Indefatigable* class (*New Zealand* and *Australia* being subscribed for by the respective dominions). Despite Fisher's boast, they were in fact, nothing more than slightly enlarged versions of *Invincible* (23 feet longer and 2 feet broader) with identical armament and speed. The only major difference being a wider diagonal siting of the midship wing turrets, which, in theory, was supposed to allow them to bring all eight 12-inch guns to bear on the broadside, as opposed to six in *Invincible*, by firing across the deck. But in practice this proved impracticable because of the gun blast, which not only damaged the deck but dazed and deafened the personnel in the turret on the engaged side of the ship.

Even before these ships were completed, the strategic situation was radically altered by the Germans' taking up the British challenge and building their own super-cruisers, which were not merely as powerful as *Invincible*, but were decidedly superior.

Almost the same length as *Invincible* (she was only four feet shorter), the 25-knot *Von der Tann* (completed in 1910) was broader and nearly 2,000 tons heavier – the extra weight being entirely devoted to a much greater amount of armour protection than had been afforded to *Invincible*. 'The thickness of armour', wrote Jellicoe, as Director of Naval Ordnance in 1905, 'is determined by the penetrative power of the projectiles likely to be used against it.' As *Invincible* had been intended to engage much weaker cruisers than herself, her light armour was not inconsistent with this criteria, but Fisher had failed to forsee the contingency of the Germans' building cruisers of comparable power. *Von der Tann*'s 6,200 tons of armour plate (which accounted for almost 30 per cent of her total displacement) and the extensive internal sub-division of the hull into watertight compartments with thick bulkheads, proved to be perfectly adequate protection against heavy-calibre projectiles. Her 10-inch thick side armour, 9-inch turret plates, and 2,000 tons of deck plating, made her an extremely tough nut to crack, in fact, practically unsinkable. In comparison, *Invincible*'s armour was woefully inadequate. Not only was it too thin (6-inch belt) to withstand heavy-calibre, armour-piercing shells, but her 3,460 tons of armour plate (20 per cent of the total displacement) wasn't as extensively and effectively distributed at it was in *Von der Tann*. The German ship's thick belt armour was carried to the ends of the ship to a far greater extent than in *Invincible* and it was carried much higher up the side of the hull.

Captain Kerr recalls that when *Invincible* was completing on the Tyne, he was visited by Sir Philip Watts, the ship designer. Kerr pointed out to him that he considered that future actions would be commenced at 15,000 yards (battle practice was still being carried out at 6,000 yards) and that a shell descending from that range would be plunging out of a high-curve trajectory, striking the ship above the armoured belt. Penetrating the unarmoured part of the hull, it would go straight down to the magazine, which would result in an explosion that would destroy the ship. According to Kerr, Watts replied that he knew the danger, but his orders were to protect the ship from a projectile fired at a range of 9,000 yards (a low trajectory in which the shell would strike the ship almost horizontally), and he was not allowed sufficient weight to put on further armour. This was another aspect of

Fisher's shortsightedness, in not appreciating that the range at which future sea battles would be fought was continually increasing, and that ranges of between 15,000 and 20,000 yards were contemplated. At these ranges, plunging fire should have been the crucial consideration.

Even more lamentable was the pathetic deck armour. Admiral Schofield remembers that when he joined *Invincible*'s sister ship *Indomitable* as a midshipman in 1912, the weakness of the deck armour was a matter of common knowledge among the officers. Beneath the thin deck plating amidships lay a transverse magazine which served the two *en echelon* wing, 12-inch gun turrets. This magazine, which lay across the full beam of the ship, contained at full load, fifty tons of high-explosive cordite and some 400 shells. Above this magazine the diesel dynamo room was sited. This was ventilated by a large air trunk to the upper deck, across which was fitted a grating, so, in fact, there was nothing to stop a plunging shell from penetrating straight through to the magazine. In a long-range action, fortune would be offered a handsome hostage. Fisher, however, was quite unperturbed, covering up the obvious weakness with slogans such as 'speed is the best protection', and 'hitting is the thing, not armour'. Dramatic phrases which in Sir Julian Corbett's words 'haunt the ear, but confuse judgement'.

The heavy weight of the defensive qualities in *Von der Tann* was obtained by a saving in weight of her offensive power. This was achieved by arming her with a lighter calibre of gun than was given to *Invincible*. Her eight 11-inch, 45 calibre guns, fired a shell of 666 pounds (184 pounds lighter than the British 12-inch). This lighter punch was accepted to ensure a ship which, in Grand Admiral Tirpitz's axiom, 'must, whatever else, be able to remain afloat and stay in action'.

Whereas the three ships of the *Indefatigable* class showed no real improvement over the *Invincibles*, the Germans followed up *Von der Tann* with armoured cruisers so powerful that they practically rendered *Invincible* obsolete. *Moltke* and *Goeben* (22,616 tons) and *Seydlitz* (24,594 tons) each carried ten 11-inch guns, and armour plate on a scale

21

equivalent to Britain's most powerful battleships. Yet it was *Derfflinger* and *Lützow* that completely outclassed *Invincible* as a fighting ship. Nearly 10,000 tons of armour, amounted to 37 per cent of their total displacement of 26,180 tons. Eight 50 calibre 12-inch guns gave them a broadside of 7,062 pounds (1,962 pounds heavier than that of *Invincible*). And a speed of 28 knots made nonsense of Fisher's slogan that 'speed is the best protection', when applied to ships that were three knots slower than their adversaries.

In view of the enormous power of the German ships, it seems incredible that the next class of large armoured cruisers that the Admiralty proposed building were to be of much the same dimensions as *Indefatigable*. However, Jellicoe in his tenure of Third Sea Lord (1908–11) realizing the folly of this, had the design altered to greatly increased size, armament and speed. The resulting ships, *Lion, Queen Mary* and *Princess Royal*, were the longest ships (700 feet) ever built in Royal Dockyards, and although they were faster (29 knots) than the German armoured cruisers, and their offensive power of eight 13.5-inch guns (10,000 pounds broadside) was enormous, their armour protection (6,200 tons or 23 per cent of the total displacement) was as lamentably thin and inadequate as that of their predecessors. This, as Professor Bryan Ranft so aptly puts it, was the direct result of 'Fisher's emotional preference for offensive war rather than rational analysis'.

'History', Fisher wrote, 'is a record of exploded ideas,' and his belief that 'speed is armour', would literally explode with the magazines of *Invincible, Indefatigable* and *Queen Mary* at Jutland.

3
Toothless Tiger
1909–1913

In the latter months of 1912, all ships of the *Invincible* type were reclassified from their original designation as 'large armoured cruisers' to that of 'battle cruisers', and in March 1913 they were formed into a Battle Cruiser Squadron, under the command of the charismatic Rear-Admiral David Beatty. This new classification was deemed necessary because the strategic role they were intended to play had radically changed. Having been designed essentially to outpace and eliminate any enemy cruisers threatening the trade routes, they were now to be employed principally as a fast wing of the battle fleet. In his report on the fleet manoeuvres of July 1913, the Commander-in-chief, Admiral Callaghan, defined the role of the Battle Cruiser Squadron as primarily *'To engage the enemy battle cruisers in a fleet action, or, if none are present, by using their speed to cross the bow of the enemy and engage the van of his battlefleet.'* They were also to act as supports to the light cruiser squadrons *'thrown out in advance of the battlefleet to prevent their being rolled up by the enemy battle cruisers'*.

Admiral of the Fleet, W. H. May, who was the umpire-in-chief of the manoeuvres, endorsed Callaghan's report with a marginal note which described the battlecruisers as *ships of the line*. Callaghan's ideas were not new. Even before she was completed Fisher was boasting that *Invincible* was in fact a 'battleship in disguise', and that with her fine speed and great gun power, she would be able to support the Battle Fleet in action by engaging the van or rear of the enemy line of battleships. When Fisher made these claims, however, all the battleships in the German fleet were old, weakly armed, lightly armoured, extremely slow pre-dreadnoughts. Now, in a fleet action, *Invincible* would find herself up against the huge, extremely powerful modern dreadnoughts of the

German navy, and battlecruisers which were, because of their enormous power, to all intents and purposes fast battleships. Ironically the Germans never officially classified their super-cruisers as anything other than armoured cruisers.

The extent of the grossly exaggerated belief in the capabilities of the battlecruisers is typified by remarks made by Winston Churchill during his tenure as First Lord of the Admiralty (1911–1915): 'At present', he wrote in June 1912, 'the British battle cruisers have an immense prestige in themselves; no one really knows their full value, it is undoubtedly great – it may even be more than we imagine . . . their speed, *their armour* [author's italics] their armament, are all great assets, even their appearance has a sobering effect'. Two months later he dispatched *Invincible* and *Indomitable*, to join up with *Inflexible* which was serving as the flagship of Admiral Milne in the Mediterranean. Together they formed the newly constituted 2nd Battle Cruiser Squadron, which was to be Britain's principal embodiment of sea power in the Mediterranean. The six battleships which had been based on Malta, were recalled to Home Waters to meet the ever-growing threat of German naval rivalry in the North Sea.

The 'traditional seat of British Imperial Power', as the Mediterranean theatre of operations was described, was to be held by the three *Invincible*s against the Italian and Austro-Hungarian battlefleets. Churchill had full confidence in them. At a meeting of the Committee of Imperial Defence, in July 1912, he announced that 'we propose to hold the Mediterranean with a force of those very large, very strong battle cruisers . . . they are units of the greatest value and strength, whose speed is so great that they need never fight unless they choose, and can always fight whenever they wish. We think this method of confronting an enemy's battle fleet by a cruiser force of the greatest strength is the best substitute for a stronger line of battle, and a far better force to have than a line of battle which is weaker than the enemy's.' This 'containing force of battle cruisers', he believed, would make 'a formidable factor for diplomatic purposes', and he was confident because of their speed that 'there is no danger of their being cut off and destroyed in detail, even if they were confronted by the most unfavourable of combinations'.

Just how ridiculous Churchill's arguments were is revealed by the knowledge, with which he was fully conversant, that all of *Invincible*'s 12-inch gun turrets were defective to the extent that she was incapable of taking offensive action and had been since her commissioning in March 1909.

In August 1905, the Admiralty decided to equip *Invincible* wth experimental electrically worked turrets. All existing naval gun mountings were hydraulically powered. Tenders from the two largest naval ordnance firms were accepted so that two alternative designs could be tried and evaluated.

Vickers supplied the fore and aft turrets ('A' and 'X') and Armstrongs, who were building the ship, the two wing midship turrets ('P' and 'Q'). Both firms signed contracts to the effect that if the electrical systems proved to be unsuccessful they would undertake to re-convert the guns to the well-tried hydraulic system.

Defects in the electric gear first came to light during the initial gun trials carried out off the Isle of Wight in October 1908. Breakdowns occurred in one or other of the hundreds of connections that existed in each turret. Each failure delayed or completely stopped the working of the turrets or loading of the guns. The violent concussion whenever the huge guns were fired put too great a strain on the delicate circuits causing shorting and breakages in the leads of the complex maze of wiring, connections and generators. To make matters worse the exact location of these kinds of defects were extremely difficult to trace. The initial defects were remedied, but more difficulties were experienced in the training and elevating gear during the second series of gun trials which took place in the Cromarty Firth in March 1909. After examination by Admiralty officials and representatives of the two firms that had supplied the mountings, a number of modifications were decided upon. During the summer of 1909, however, more defects were discovered and if the ship had been required to go into action only four of *Invincible*'s 12-inch guns would have been effective while the other four could only have been worked at a rate considerably slower than was regarded as efficient. This was obviously an unsatisfactory state of affairs.

In August 1909 *Invincible* was taken in hand at Portsmouth dockyard for further modifications to be effected and by the third week of November the turrets were believed to be ready for trial. During this period the ship was held at a fortnight's notice, but it was discovered that the gear was still not satisfactory and further modifications were decided on which were completed by the end of December. But even after all these alterations the electrical appliances for the turrets still proved faulty with the result that *Invincible* did not fire her guns (two full charges from each) until 22 February 1910. This was the first time that she had fired a 12-inch shell since the trials carried out in the Cromarty Firth in early March 1909, almost a year previously.

The results of the February 1910 trials were not encouraging and the electrical fittings continued to prove defective. A final attempt to put things right was undertaken at the contractor's own cost when *Invincible* paid off at Portsmouth on 27 March 1911 for a three-month refit. Once again the adjustment and alterations failed to alleviate the trouble and the Admiralty finally had to admit that the experiment had failed; conceding that 'the design of the electric appliances for working the turrets, etc., in this vessel are faulty and it is improbable that they would ever be made to work satisfactorily without redesign and replacement'.

The final decision to abandon the abortive experiment and re-convert *Invincible*'s gun mountings to the reliable hydraulic system was made at a conference held at the Admiralty on 20 March 1912. The Director of Naval Ordnance, Captain A. G. Moore, estimated that the conversion would take six months to complete and would cost £150,000. The docking of the ship was scheduled for October 1912, but was cancelled because of *Invincible*'s impending Mediterranean transfer. And so it was that a ship, almost totally devoid of offensive power, a defect the more grievous given her weak defensive qualities, was dispatched as an integral portion of the 'containing force' which was to protect Britain's vital maritime interest in politically unstable waters.

In her impotent state *Invincible* remained in the Mediterranean until 10 December 1913 when she was recalled to Home Waters, her place in the 2nd Battle Cruiser Squadron being taken by *Indefatigable*. She arrived at Portsmouth on 13 December and was immediately paid off into dockyard hands to begin a refit which would last eight months. Meanwhile, war clouds were gathering over Europe.

4

Action!
The Battle of the Bight,
August 1914

At 11.00 p.m. (midnight by German time) on 4 August 1914, the Admiralty flashed the signal to all ships flying the White Ensign 'Commence hostilities against Germany.' The First World War had begun. In the northern mists the Grand Fleet (21 dreadnoughts, 8 predreadnoughts, 4 battlecruisers, 21 cruisers and 42 destroyers) was at its war base in Scapa Flow, under the command of Admiral Jellicoe. Diagonally across the North Sea the German High Seas Fleet (13 dreadnoughts, 16 predreadnoughts, 4 battlecruisers, 18 cruisers and 88 destroyers) were assembling in the River Jade under the command of Admiral Von Ingenohl.

The outbreak of hostilities found *Invincible* still in dockyard hands at Portsmouth. She had been re-commissioned into service by Captain Charles de Bartolome on 3 August, but 2,000 dockyard men were still working around the clock to complete the conversion of the gun turrets to hydraulic power and get the ship fully operational as quickly as possible. On Monday the 5th, 1,100 officers and men of the ship's company, who had assembled at the Royal Naval Barracks, joined the ship. Lieutenant-Commander Barry Bingham remembered that '. . . a more hopeless looking ship than the *Invincible* I never wish to behold or commission again. Moored alongside the North Railway jetty the Battle Cruiser was prey to some 2,000 grimy, oily dockyard mateys who were working like a swarm of ants in all parts of the ship. Streaming backwards and forwards between jetty and pier, some were carrying huge loads on their backs, others were crawling up ladders and through turrets: one and all jostling each other in feverish activity. The noise was indescribable. Night and day their hammering riveting and plate-burning went on continuously.'

While the dockyard work continued apace the newly berthed crew set about coaling ship and hoisting in ammunition and cordite to plenish the magazines. The ship was finally declared seaworthy and operational on the 12th of the month. On the same day, Rear-Admiral Sir Archibald Gordon Moore hoisted his flag in *Invincible*. Four days later she put to sea bound for the naval base at Queenstown on the south coast of Ireland. Fearful that the enemy battlecruisers might attempt to break out into the Atlantic to attack the trade routes, the Admiralty considered that basing *Invincible* on Queenstown would put her in an ideal position to intercept them.

Once the ship had sailed, gunnery experts from the Royal Naval Gunnery School (HMS 'Excellent') supervised a gunnery trial. Each 12-inch gun was fired and tested separately with a few rounds until the gunnery staff were satisfied that the newly installed hydraulic motivating-gear was functioning properly. The experts might have been satisfied, but Bingham was far from happy. 'The trouble lay', he wrote, 'with the valves and pipes, which leaked and continued to leak unceasingly. At my battle station in "A", or the foremost turret, I found two outer garments indispensable: to wit, overalls to protect myself against the dirt and a mackintosh to resist the water from the valves, which, as soon as pressure was turned on, streamed in one continual deluge, comparable only to a perpetual shower-bath.'

On completion of the gunnery trials, *Invincible* anchored in the Dale Roads off Milford Haven to top up with 480 tons of Welsh coal and disembark the gunnery experts. While she was at Milford the Germans launched a raid by two fast light cruisers on the destroyer patrol watching the Broad Fourteens off the Dutch coast.

Worried lest the Germans repeat the raid with battlecruisers, the Admiralty decided that *Invincible* and *New Zealand*, together with three light cruisers, should be based on the Humber, from where they were to act as a powerful advanced cruiser force, to support the Broad Fourteens patrol (two destroyer flotillas and five old armoured cruisers, the latter not having fired their guns for years). This patrol was watching the approaches to the Straits of Dover to give early warning of any attempt by the Germans to attack the troop transports regularly crossing over to France and Belgium. An Admiralty signal to Rear-Admiral Moore instructed him to keep in communication with the Rear-Admiral in command of the patrol forces 'to know how and when support will be required'. And although it was 'their Lordships' wish not to have the valuable Battle Cruisers unduly risked', they were to attempt to cut off the retreat of the enemy should a repetition of the raid of 18 August be attempted. One can readily imagine what would have happened if *Invincible* and *New Zealand* had tried to cut off the retreat of the four vastly superior German battlecruisers if they had acted in concert.

Having sailed from Milford during the evening of 19 August, and narrowly missing collision with a tramp steamer in the English Channel during the night, *Invincible* anchored off Grimsby in the River Humber on Saturday the 22nd. On the following morning she was joined by *New Zealand*, which had been detached from the 1st Battle Cruiser Squadron at Scapa.

Another gunnery trial was carried out off the Humber with ¾ charges and practice shell from the 12-inch guns on the morning of the following Wednesday (25th). According to Sub-Lieutenant Stewart, the Loading Officer in 'A' turret '. . . everything that possibly could go wrong with the hydraulic system did so'. He also found the accuracy (*Invincible* had dropped a target) 'very disappointing'. To iron out these defects was imperative because *Invincible* and *New Zealand*, now designated as Cruiser Force 'K', had been ordered (Admiralty signal to Rear-Admiral Moore on the 25th) to support a sweep by two destroyer flotillas into the Heligoland Bight, which was to commence in the early hours of Friday, 28 August.

British submarines, which had been reconnoitring the Bight since the outbreak of the war, had recorded in detail the movements of the enemy destroyer patrols operating in the area. The plan called for the 1st Flotilla (sixteen destroyers) and the 3rd Flotilla (fifteen destroyers), both led by a light cruiser, to reach a point thirty miles south-west of the Horn Reefs lightship off the Danish coast under the cover of darkness. At 4.00 a.m. they were to sweep south towards the island of Heligoland, and at 8.00 a.m., when the force would be a few miles north-west of Heligoland, they were to turn west, spread out on a nine-mile front and sweep towards Terschelling, cutting off and falling upon the German destroyer patrols.

Invincible and *New Zealand* were to lend heavy support from a position forty miles north-west of Heligoland, but the Admiralty were banking on all of the heavy units of the High Seas Fleet being tide-bound behind the River Jade's outer bar, which large ships could not clear at low water, until the sweep was well under way. (High water did not occur until noon.) Jellicoe learned of the operation on the afternoon of the 26th. He considered the force too weak in the event of any German heavy ships being at sea and not, as anticipated, tide-bound in the Jade, and he suggested co-operating with the entire Grand Fleet. The Admiralty vetoed the suggestion, but replied that Beatty's three remaining battlecruisers at Scapa 'can support if convenient'.

Screened by four destroyers, *Invincible* and *New Zealand*, left Grimsby at 10.30 a.m. on the 27th and shaped course at fifteen knots for the support position, passing the Outer Dowsing lightship at 1.18 p.m. According to Sub-Lieutenant Stewart, Captain Bartolome had addressed the ship's company before sailing, informing them that they would undoubtedly be in action within the next twenty-four hours, although he gave no clue as to their destination. At 4.00 a.m. on the following morning *Invincible* sighted Beatty's battlecruisers (*Lion, Queen Mary* and *Princess Royal*) which had hurried down from Scapa, having sailed five hours before *Invincible* left Grimsby, and took station on *Lion*'s starboard beam at 4.45 a.m.

Approaching the Bight on a southerly course, the five battlecruisers marked time in the support position by navigating a complete circle from 8.00 a.m. to 9.30 a.m. They maintained a position roughly north-west of Heligoland by steaming south-west at 24 knots for an hour and then backtracking on a north-easterly course at sixteen knots until 11.00 a.m., zigzagging to avoid submarine attack.

The sea was calm. Patches of mist reduced visibility to 3,000 yards in places. Everything was quiet. Two signals (8.15 and 9.41 a.m.) from the light forces informed Beatty and Moore that they were in action with the enemy. Thereafter they could only guess at what was actually happening in the mist to the east. Then, at 11.25 a.m., the battlecruisers received an urgent message from Commodore Tyrwhitt, who was leading the sweep in the light cruiser *Arethusa*, requesting urgent assistance, followed by another two signals in quick succession (11.28 and 11.30 a.m.) repeating the need for assistance and adding that he was 'hard pressed'.

The plan had gone awry. The 3rd Flotilla had come into contact with the German destroyer patrols shortly after the sweep southward into the Bight had commenced (6.53 a.m.). After a confused action in thick mist, they sank one German destroyer and damaged three others. They then lost sight of the German patrols, which retired at high speed to Heligoland and the Jade, and instead found themselves in action with a hornets' nest of enemy light cruisers which the German Fleet command sent out to cover the retirement of their flotillas. With his forces scattered over a wide area in the ever-thickening mist, running short of ammunition and with *Arethusa* and three destroyers seriously damaged, Tyrwitt was in grave danger of suffering a crushing defeat.

Despite the serious risk of running into mines, attack by hostile submarines and the possibility that the Germans had a superior force of heavy ships in the area, Beatty, relying on the high speed of the battlecruisers to get him out of trouble, discounted the dangers and at 11.35 turned east-south-east and ordered the battlecruisers to steam at full speed to cover the forty odd miles which lay between him and the hard-pressed destroyer flotillas.

When the order to steam headlong into the Bight was given, *Invincible* and *New Zealand* were slightly ahead of *Lion* and on her port bow, but as Beatty's three great ships worked up to their full speed of 28 knots they quickly overtook Moore's two older, slower ships. By 12.42 *New Zealand* was lagging behind the leading ships and *Invincible* had fallen behind her. (In an earlier signal to Beatty, Moore stated that 'The *Invincible* might do 25 knots for a short time.')

Assistant Paymaster Gordon Franklyn remembers that '. . . it was just after noon that action was sounded on the *Invincible* – the first time any of us had ever heard the stirring call blown (on a bugle) in earnest. Sounds of firing could be heard to the North West and half an hour later the *Arethusa* and the 3rd Flotilla were sighted in action with an enemy Light Cruiser.'

By the time *Lion* opened fire (12.50) *Invincible* had fallen behind by two miles, so that it was Beatty's three ships which stole all the thunder, and by the time *Invincible* came into range all the enemy light cruisers had been scattered and sent fleeing into the mist. Two of them, the *Mainz* and the *Ariadne*, had been reduced to burning, sinking wrecks. The only remaining target presenting itself to *Invincible* was the light cruiser, *Cöln*, on fire and limping away to the north. Swinging out of line, *Invincible* altered course to port to chase the fleeing *Cöln* which was steering north-east on the fringe of the mist. At 1.10 p.m. *Invincible* fired her guns for the first time in anger. Although the range was short (5,000 yards) none of the eighteen shells she fired found the target. *Cöln*'s northerly course led her back onto the guns of the other battlecruisers which had turned north and circled around to port. They immediately opened fire at 4,000 yards, once more robbing *Invincible* of a kill. Gordon Franklyn says that . . . 'Those ten minutes (of the cannonade) must have been hell for the poor wretches on board, as our Squadron's big guns literally raked her fore and aft. She quickly caught fire, turned over and sank with her colours flying' (1.35 p.m.). Destroyers were sent to pick up survivors but they found none. (One survivor from *Cöln*'s crew of 506 was in fact picked up by a German destroyer two days later.)

As the battlecruisers covered the retirement of the destroyer flotillas westward, *Invincible* finally caught up (2.30 p.m.) and took station astern of *New Zealand*. Twenty minutes earlier the German battlecruisers had crossed the outer Jade bar (low water was between 7.00 a.m. and noon).

Half-heartedly they scouted a short distance to the west and finding nothing returned to harbour.

Gordon Franklyn relates how, at the close of the action, the Ship's Company ran up onto the deck of Invincible cheering, 'delighted in having been blooded'. They hadn't scored a hit on the enemy, neither had *Cöln*, their only adversary, returned their fire with her puny 4.1-inch guns. But their elation in having taken part in what *The Times* of the following day described as 'A Brilliant Naval Action', is understandable. Churchill (First Lord of the Admiralty) was equally elated, describing the action as 'a fine feat of arms — vindicated by success'. No one bothered to question why it took 197 tons of high-explosive shells (284 13.5-inch and 101 12-inch) to sink three small cruisers at almost point-blank range (4,000 to 5,000 yards). The poor shooting of the battlecruisers was partly to blame, mitigated in itself by the poor visibility, but the real reason, which did not present itself to those concerned, was that the shells were defective. Instead of penetrating into the vitals of the ship before bursting, as they were designed to do, the majority broke up on impact causing mainly superficial damage. 'We thus lost', Jellicoe wrote after the war, 'the advantage we ought to have enjoyed in *offensive* power due to the greater weight of our projectiles, while suffering the disadvantages in the (weak) protection of our ships due to the heavy weights of our guns and ammunition which reduced the total weight available for armour plating.' Ill-equipped to take a punch, it now transpired that *Invincible* couldn't throw a proper punch either.

At 4.35 p.m., when the whole force was clear of the Bight, *Invincible* and *New Zealand*, with their four screening destroyers, parted company with Beatty's Squadron (bound for Scapa) and turned south to support the old armoured cruisers patrolling on the Broad Fourteens in case German big ships prowled this far in search of the forces retiring from the Bight.

Meanwhile, a minefield (laid by the German minelayer *Nautilus* on the night of 25–26 August) had been discovered just north of the Outer Dowsing lightship. Because of the difficulties in defining the extent of the minefield it was decided that the Humber was no longer tenable as a base for the battlecruisers and at 2.20 p.m. on 29 August the Admiralty ordered Rear-Admiral Moore to proceed to Rosyth which was to be the future base of Cruiser Force 'K'. *Invincible*'s log records that she 'came to' in the Forth River at Rosyth at 8.17 a.m. on the morning of Sunday 30 August. Six days later the two battlecruisers were joined at Rosyth by *Lion, Princess Royal* and *Queen Mary*, together with *Inflexible* which had returned from the Mediterranean. She took *New Zealand*'s place in Cruiser Force 'K'; *New Zealand*, being a faster ship, joining the 1st Battle Cruiser Squadron.

On the evening of Monday 7 September the six battlecruisers put to sea in single line ahead, having 'a hearty send off as they passed under the Forth Railway Bridge', proceeding at a steady fifteen knots to a position in the North Sea 100 miles East of Peterhead. They cruised in this area during the daylight hours of the 8th, turning south that night towards Heligoland.

The Admiralty had decided to have another go at 'bighting the Bight'. From German prisoners taken during the action of 28 August, it was learned that the German battlecruisers had been preparing to come out in support of their light cruisers. The Admiralty now hoped that a repetition of the raid would draw out at least some of the enemy's heavy ships. This time, apart from the close support of the battlecruisers forty miles north-west of Heligoland, Jellicoe was ordered to bring the whole of the Grand Fleet down to within 100 miles of Heligoland in case the High Seas Fleet, or a portion of it, put to sea.

Sub-Lieutenant Stewart recalls that as *Invincible* steamed South on the evening of the 9th, 'The Commander (Richard Townsend) cleared the lower deck and informed the Ship's Company that we would probably be in action early in the morning. We were all to sleep in our clothes, in case we were attacked during the night, and great care was to be taken in darkening the ship. As far as I can make out the show is the same as last time, only we are to wait on the scene and not

35

withdraw, in the hope that some of their battle fleet will come out, in which case Jellicoe with the Grand Fleet will swoop down and get behind them.'

The sweep southwards into the Bight by the destroyers began at 2.30 a.m. on the morning of 10 September. Once again mist reduced visibility to a maximum of four miles; for much of the time it was far less. When the force turned westward (3.45 a.m.), they passed within a few miles of the German 3rd Flotilla steering north, but in the mist neither side sighted the other. Bitterly disappointed that the sweep had proved abortive, the battlecruisers turned North at 7.30 a.m. to rendezvous with the Grand Fleet sixty miles north-east of their position.

The battle fleet was sighted from *Invincible* at 10.45 a.m. 'It was a wonderful sight that day,' Gordon Franklyn relates, 'when after all hopes of a "scrap" had been abandoned, practically the whole striking force of the navy assembled in a few square miles of the North Sea, and then proceeded to manoeuvre and exercise. The ordinary Spithead Review, with the ships anchored in seemingly endless lines, is impressive enough, but here, with the flower of the Empire's naval might cleared for action, was a scene to baffle adequate description.'

At noon the whole fleet fanned out on a broad front and swept northwards with the object of intercepting any warships or merchant ships with goods destined for Germany. *Invincible* and *Inflexible* occupied the left flank with six minesweepers spread out ahead of them. They arrived at Scapa at 9.00 a.m. on the 12th.

As the danger of mines had rendered the Humber untenable as a base for Cruiser Force 'K', and Rosyth was too far north for Rear-Admiral Moore effectively to support the Broad Fourteen patrols, it was decided to integrate *Invincible* and *Inflexible* into the Grand Fleet under the title of the 2nd Battle Cruiser Squadron.

5

The Fury of the Gale
The Only Enemy

On the afternoon of 3 October 1914, *Invincible* and *Inflexible* in the company of two armed merchant cruisers (*Alsatian* and *Teutonic*), three minelayers and the old Cruiser *Sappho*, sailed from Scapa to take up a patrol line north of the Shetlands. Intelligence reports had reached the Admiralty that two armed German Liners (*Prince Friedrich Wilhelm* and *Brandenburg*, both known to be in Norwegian ports) were preparing to break out into the Atlantic to attack a convoy of Canadian troops crossing to the battlefields in France from Halifax in 31 liners. The Admiralty was also apprehensive that the Germans might send out their battle-cruisers to attack this tempting target. While *Invincible* steamed north the Grand Fleet deployed to secure an iron grip on the North Sea.

The weather on the night of the 3rd was foul. Gordon Franklyn records that: 'Our duffel coats and balaclavas were very welcome. Day had ended with a vivid sunset, blood-red storm-clouds scudded across the face of the sun as it sank below the horizon. For a time a watery moon fitfully shone through the racing clouds, to be gradually blotted out by the rolling greyness. Then, in the inky darkness the chill nor'easter each moment blew stronger as the *Invincible*, dipping her nose into the sea, "took it green" over the length of the forecastle, the spray and spume reaching right up to the massive height of the bridge. Eight bells struck – midnight. Muffled forms laboriously made their way up to the bridge, clinging for dear life to ladder or stanchion as they met the full force of the wind, tucking their chins further into the necks of their duffel coats as the spray lashed them. From different spots in the pitch blackness scraps of hurried conversation drifted astern; the watch going off duty were turning over to reliefs.'

For ten days *Invincible* and her consorts pounded into the heaving seas of the grey North Atlantic. Such conditions made life extremely uncomfortable for everyone aboard. The perpetual rolling and lurching, extreme in *Invincible*'s case as she was declared to be a bad sea boat, made every activity difficult and taxing. 'For ten days out of a clear-cut black horizon the north-easter blew,' wrote Gordon Franklyn. 'For ten days we bucketed about amid waves that hourly seemed to grow bigger and more awe-inspiring; for ten days, chilled to the bone, we gazed out on the incessant white flurry of a grey and white sea – the whole now dull and ominous-looking under a rolling dark sky, now sparkling steely, greeny black as a brilliant sun lit up its crests and furrows; one day driving our nose into the foam-capped combers, the next riding comparatively easily with the tumult astern. Then came the looked-for gentle rise of the glass, but it brought us, not as we hoped, the climax of the gale before the calm, but biting villainous hail and rain.' During the whole ten days they saw nothing but the storm-lashed sea. The German ships remained in harbour, the convoy of 33,000 Canadian troops crossing the Atlantic unmolested. 'We anchored in Scapa Flow at 7.00 a.m. on Thursday the 13th October', wrote Sub-Lieutenant Stewart, 'and immediately prepared for coaling. Colliers came in on each side of us. We had 2,050 tons to take in. Coaling finished at 11.30 p.m. One poor fellow, a new petty officer, broke his back in number 4 hold: two bags of coal falling on him.'

On the afternoon of 16 October, while Lieutenant-Commander Bingham and Sub-Lieutenant Stewart were enjoying a walk ashore, they suddenly noticed an unusual amount of activity among the fleet anchored in the Flow. At *Invincible*'s yards the *general recall* signal was flying. They arrived back onboard, via a picket boat, as two colliers were being secured along each side of the battlecruiser. A submarine had been reported inside the Flow and the colliers were intended to act as buffers against the danger of torpedoes. Three reports of the submarine were made (Switha Battery 4.00 p.m., the destroyer *Shark* 4.18, and *Invincible* reported seeing a periscope off her starboard side at 5.20). Although Jellicoe was inclined to dismiss the sightings as false ('probably a seal', was his laconic remark in the *Grand Fleet Narrative*), he could take no chances and ordered the fleet to raise steam with all dispatch and proceed to sea. *Invincible* and *Inflexible* got under way at 8.30 p.m., followed a short while later by the entire Grand Fleet.

Wags in the fleet called the incident the 'second battle of Scapa Flow' (a similar incident had occurred on 1 September). 'Guns were fired, destroyers thrashed the waters, and the whole gigantic Armada put to sea in haste and dudgeon,' was Churchill's caustic assessment.

While the battle fleet sought temporary sanctuary in Lough Swilly on the north coast of Ireland, *Invincible* and *Inflexible* were instructed to patrol between Flannen Island and Sole Skerry to intercept trade. At 7.30 p.m. on the following day, Rear-Admiral Moore received a signal from the Admiralty ordering him to proceed to Cromarty after dark on the 19th, and fill up with coal, his squadron being required to support yet another operation by light forces in the Bight.

This time the plan called for two light cruisers and sixteen destroyers to screen two seaplane carriers which were to launch a seaplane bombing raid on the Zeppelin sheds at Cuxhaven. As a diversion the light cruiser *Fearless* and ten destroyers were to sweep eastwards seven miles off the western Ems at 4.00 a.m., advertising their presence by firing a few rounds from their guns.

After taking in 1,000 tons of coal at Cromarty, *Invincible* led *Inflexible* and four screening destroyers to sea on the night of the 23rd. 'Midnight and again at sea,' Gordon Franklyn complained. 'Rough weather too. Just as we were congratulating ourselves on at least one more night in harbour. Now, here we are well away from the lee of the land, the *Invincible* staggering and rolling as she runs with the fury of the gale on her starboard beam. In the inky blackness the gale shrieks, whistles and groans.'

Early the following morning, Commodore Tyrwhitt, leading the light forces into the Bight, signalled to Moore that the raid would have to be postponed for 24 hours due to the unfavourable weather. Moore, to avoid disclosing his movements to the enemy, accordingly turned the battlecruisers north and cruised to the north of the 59th parallel (about 100 miles east of the Orkneys) before turning south again, to reach the support position 65 miles NW of Heligoland at 6 a.m. on the morning of Sunday the 25th.

Marine Corporal Albert Lee serving in *Inflexible* recalls that '. . . We were steaming SE at fourteen knots. The destroyers were having a rough time of it in the heavy seas that were running. at 11.30 a.m. (24th) we received the following signal from the *Invincible*: "The present operations may result in a Cruiser action at any time after 6.00 a.m. Ships are to be fully prepared for general action at that hour. It is doubtful if guns crews will be able to leave their guns for breakfast. Arrangements must be made accordingly." '

When they reached the support position it was raining heavily and visibility was down to one mile. Once again disappointment was to be their only reward, the operation was aborted. The seaplanes could not take off because of the weather, and at 7.30 a.m. the forces involved fell back on the battlecruisers which supported their retirement westwards until they were clear of Terschelling.

Meanwhile 9,000 miles away, on the western seaboard of South America, events were taking place that would give *Invincible*'s crew the glory they craved.

6

The Greyhounds Unleashed
In Search of Von Spee

Thursday, 5 November 1914, found *Invincible* and *Inflexible* at anchor in the Cromarty Firth. Sub-Lieutenant Stewart's diary has the following entry for that day: 'Received news that Admiral Sturdee was to hoist his flag in *Invincible*. Admiral Moore to shift his flag to *New Zealand*. *Invincible* and *Inflexible* to go to Devonport at once. We first of all thought that we were booked for the Mediterranean, but later received the following signal from Cromarty: "Unofficial. *Monmouth* and *Good Hope* attacked off Valparaiso by German ships. *Monmouth* sunk all hands lost. *Good Hope* ran ashore in burning condition. *Glasgow* seriously damaged but is thought she was able to make for the nearest port. The report comes from the Germans and therefore must not be accepted as reliable." '

Sadly, in its essentials, the report was true. During the evening of 1 November, Rear-Admiral Sir Christopher Cradock, with a weak cruiser squadron consisting of two old armoured cruisers (*Good Hope* and *Monmouth*), a modern light cruiser (*Glasgow*) and an armed merchant cruiser (*Otranto*), had run into the German East Asiatic Squadron, under the command of the aggressive Vice-Admiral Graf von Spee, 50 miles west of Coronel. With a superior force (the powerful modern armoured cruisers *Scharnhorst* and *Gneisenau*, and three light cruisers – *Leipzig*, *Nürnberg* and *Dresden*), skilful tactics and extraordinary gunnery, Spee sank Cradock's two armoured cruisers without suffering any appreciable damage (his two armoured cruisers were hit only six times in total, without effect). *Glasgow* (only slightly damaged) and *Otranto* managed to escape under cover of darkness.

'Putting two and two together,' wrote Stewart, 'we came to the conclusion that we were obviously going out to settle things.' Fisher, who had been recalled out of retirement to fill the post of First Sea Lord on 29 October (he was 74), was the prime mover, having decided within an hour of the receipt of the news of the defeat at Coronel, to dispatch the two battlecruisers (his beloved greyhounds of the sea) to retrieve the situation. It was a force, he believed, that would annihilate Spee, not merely beat him. It was, after all, expressly for the purpose of destroying enemy marauding cruisers that he had designed and built *Invincible* in the first place. And Von Spee's reason for operating off South America was to attack the important trade routes in the area.

Parathentically, the other *raison d'être* of *Invincible* – to counter the threat of armed German liners – proved to be rather a non-starter. Of the 42 liners capable of being converted to auxiliaries, only five were commissioned for service, and only three actually got onto the trade routes. They netted 29 Allied merchant ships (104,629 tons, which was less than 1 per cent of the total mercantile tonnage), before being sunk or interned in neutral ports.

Rear-Admiral Moore and his staff disembarked from *Invincible* at noon, and at 6.55 p.m. the two battlecruisers, *Inflexible* leading, steamed out of the Cromarty Firth at seventeen knots on the first leg of their great adventure. *Invincible* was now under the command of Tufton Percy Hamilton Beamish, who had relieved Bartolome on 3 November. North they went, then west through the Pentland Firth between Stroma and the Pentland Skerries south of Scapa Flow, then south-west past Cape Wrath, sighting the Butt of Lewis on the Outer Hebrides on the afternoon of 6 November, then south through the Irish Channel. 'That night,' Stewart relates, 'we sighted a vessel without lights and she didn't answer when we challenged her. All gun crews closed up, we put on full speed and closed her, intending to open fire if she didn't answer the challenge. Luckily for her she answered just in time. It turned out to be one of our cruisers.'

The Eddystone light was sighted at 5.02 a.m. on the morning of the 8th. A thick fog had descended by the time they entered Plymouth Sound and they had to anchor inside the breakwater and wait for a pilot before navigating up river to Devonport dockyard. On route *Inflexible* grounded on a sandbar, delaying the docking of the two ships until the afternoon (*Invincible* 1.57 p.m., *Inflexible* 3.00 p.m.).

Invincible went straight into No. 9 dry dock to have the bottom of her hull scraped clean (a clean hull would give her an extra knot or two of speed). Dockyard officials examined the ship, and on the following morning the Commander-in-Chief of the dockyard (Admiral George Egerton) sent a wire to the Admiralty stating that 'The earliest possible date of completion (of repairs) to *Invincible* and *Inflexible* is midnight November 13th. The brick boilers of *Invincible* cannot be finished before.' Fisher, irate over the delay, prodded Churchill into shooting back a stinger to Egerton: '*Invincible* and *Inflexible* are needed for War Service and are to sail Wednesday 11th November. Dockyard arrangements must be made to conform. You are held responsible for the speedy dispatch of these ships in a thoroughly efficient condition. If necessary dockyard men should be sent away in the ships, to return as opportunity offers.'

At 7.00 p.m. that same day, Monday the 9th, Midshipman Allan McEwan joined *Invincible*, having been transferred from the cruiser *Diana*. 'The *Invincible* was in dry dock,' he recorded in his diary, 'her decks stacked with stores and provisions. At first I was lost in such a large ship. On Tuesday 10th we (the midshipmen) ran up to the baths at the barracks and enjoyed a good swim. After breakfast we were sent on shore to buy new gear. We were not allowed to keep our sea chests, so tin trunks had to be acquired. It was quite a question whether we would be able to get our whites in time. We were given leave from 4 to 11.30 p.m. There isn't much to do in Plymouth now after 9 p.m. for all the shops shut then and the street lamps are all put out. On returning on board, the *Invincible* had been moved out of the dock to the coaling jetty. We shifted into coaling rig and started coaling just before midnight. We coaled ship till 11.30 a.m. the following morning, with a break for cocoa about 3 a.m. and breakfast at 7.30 a.m. We took in 1,500 tons.'

On the completion of coaling, Assistant Paymaster Clement Woodland, RNR (who joined the ship on 8

November) supervised the provisioning of the ship. He kept a record of the intake in his diary: Spirits 13,388 pints; Flour 134,396 pounds; Biscuits 2,749 pounds; Fresh meat 15,251 pounds; Vegetables 26,180 pounds; Milk 15,434 pounds; Sugar 37,875 pounds; Tea 4,392 pounds; Coffee 911 pounds; Chocolate 4,253 pounds; Jams and marmalade 10,166 pounds; Preserved meat 19,735 pounds; Pickles 3,070 pounds; Rabbit 2,872 pounds; Salmon 6,251 pounds; Mustard 451 pounds; Pepper 364 pounds; Salt 3,136 pounds; Vinegar 3,003 pounds; Salt pork 9,388 pounds; Split peas 4,943 pounds; Celery 560 pounds; Suet 2,398 pounds; Raisins 3,245 pounds; rice 3,320 pounds; Lime juice 2,212 pounds; Oatmeal 480 pounds; Haricot beans 8,111 pounds; Marrowfat peas 12,406 pounds; Hops 58 pounds; Malt 680 pounds; Lard 120 pounds.

At noon on the 11th, Vice-Admiral Sir Frederick Charles Doveton Sturdee hoisted his flag in *Invincible*. The fifty-five year-old Sturdee ('Short in stature, jutting jaw, prominent Roman nose, with heavy brows above deep, close-set eyes') was a man of great sea experience, with a reputation for being deeply read in tactics, history and war. He was generally disliked by his compatriots who found him pedantic and conceited. Fisher, in particular, detested him, blaming him (he had just been relieved as Chief-of-Staff by the irascible Sea Lord) for the faulty dispositions which resulted in the defeat at Coronel. 'Never such utter rot', Fisher wrote to Beatty (19 November), 'as perpetrated by Sturdee in his world-wide dispersal of weak units! Strong nowhere, weak everywhere!' Fisher gave Sturdee command of the 'two greyhounds' to give the 'pedantic ass' a chance to redeem himself. His orders (dated 9 November) were to proceed to St. Vincent, Cape Verde Islands, where he was to coal, and thence to South American waters where he was to rendezvous with Rear-Admiral Stoddart's 5th Cruiser Squadron at the Abrolhos Rocks (off the *Brazilian* coast) and then search out von Spee; his main duty being to bring the *Scharnhorst* and *Gneisenau* to action.

'We left harbour at 4.45 a.m.,' Woodland wrote. 'I remained on deck until we had passed the harbour boom. It had been reported that German submarines were outside but none were seen. A strong breeze was blowing and it was cold and rough.

Thursday, 12 November
(Woodland's diary)
'Got up at noon, shaved and dressed with difficulty and got on deck. I was not very sick, but felt rotten. Ate a few dry biscuits and went to bed at 1 o'clock.'

(McEwan's diary)
'We were well into the "Bay", and a South Westerly swell with a strong wind made the upper deck and poop an impossible place to stand without getting wet.'

Friday, 13 November
(Woodland's diary)
'Feeling much better and managed to eat a good breakfast. We are now off Portugal. The *Inflexible* is steaming on a parallel course. Spent part of the morning in the decoding office, seeing how this work is done. At 10.00 a.m. all officers on deck to be introduced to the Admiral. He spoke a few words to me personally. Tea at 4.00 p.m. Afterwards played deck-hockey on the starboard side of the upper deck. Dinner at 7.00 p.m., then read and smoked.

My cabin is excellent, about 14 by 8 ft and contains bed, my cot on the floor, two chest of drawers, writing table, two chairs. Beyond it is an inner room containing large bath, two wash hand stands, two mirrors and WC. A geyser gives us hot water at any time. I'm sharing with Captain Malden of the Marines who is in charge of the wireless. Today the weather has been good and the sea, which is becoming a deeper blue, very calm.

Saturday, 14 November
(Woodland's diary)
'Strenuous game of deck-hockey after tea. Much warmer, sea calm, sky cloudy. Passed a liner about 2.00 p.m., probably White Star from Australia. We are now opposite Madeira. Menus:-
Breakfast- Porridge, fish patties, eggs and bacon.

Lunch-   Bread, butter, jam and cakes.
Dinner- Soup, salt beef, maccaroni cheese, dessert and coffee.'

Sunday, 15 November
(Woodland's diary)
'At 10.00 a.m. all on deck while Captain inspected ship. At 11.00 a.m. Church Service in the marines' messroom, a good simple service. Very much warmer, but nice breeze, little sunshine.'

Monday, 16 November
(Woodland's diary)
'During the morning I went on deck to watch target practice and met the Commander (Richard Townsend), who asked me why I was not at action stations! I told him I had no station! He told me to go in future at action stations in the Sick Bay. I find my place will be in a small room down below! Today I saw a flying-fish. Hockey in the evening. A glorious sunset. It is pleasantly warm. It was funny to see the two fore 12-inch guns used to support a big sail for a bathing pool! Worked on provision books. Wrote a letter home.'

(McEwan's diary)
'The *Inflexible* closed and practised sub-calibre firing at the target we towed. It was very wild at first, for one shot went over our main derrick. Deck-hockey as usual in the 1st Dog Watch. Today we went into half whites. In the evening a swimming bath was rigged forrad of "A" turret.'

Tuesday, 17 November
(Woodland's diary)
'A glorious day. I sat for a long time this afternoon on deck in the sun. We are now in full white uniform. The flying-fish are most interesting; they appear like small flocks of birds; none are very large, the largest about the size of medium herring.
   Soon after 3.00 p.m. the Cape Verde Islands (off the West coast of Africa) appeared in sight. St. Antonio Point was actually sighted at 2.20 p.m. As we approached, I noticed about five islands. On our starboard we passed a large island probably Sao Antao (8,000 feet), it rose straight up from the

sea, the top being covered with cloud. It appeared quite desolate, obviously of volcanic origin, as I could see distinct craters. No sign of any vegetation or trees. We anchored at Porto Grande in Sao Vincent. The port is in a big bay in the form of a semicircle.

Many ships in harbour including one of own armed merchantmen *The Victorian*, of the Allan Line, a Portuguese gun boat and about eight German steamers. We fired two salutes — 20 and 15 rounds — which were replied to by the gun boat. We soon had many small boats round us bringing the Consul, Harbour Master, natives with green oranges, bananas, coral necklaces, etc. A collier was soon alongside and we commenced coaling at 8.33 p.m. It was a fine sight as we saluted — the sun was sinking and threw the bleak base island out in bold relief.'

(McEwan's diary)
'At 5.15 p.m. we anchored with five shackles of cable out from the port anchor. About 8.30 p.m. the first collier came alongside the starboard side, and coaling commenced. Soon after midnight the second collier came alongside the port side. With breaks for cocoa, breakfast and lunch, coaling went on till 2.30 p.m. the following day. It was slow working in the heat and sun, which were the hottest we've had.'

Wednesday, 18 November
(Diary of Marine Corporal Albert Lee, HMS Inflexible)
'At 1.30 a.m. Boy Telegrapher Stewart was killed whilst attending the whip of No. I starboard motor during coaling. Death must have been instantaneous. He was completely taken round the drum. This was his first ship. He joined us a week ago at Devonport. He was only 16 and 2 months old. 11.00 a.m. Commander N. and Lieutenant-Commander T. held an enquiry. There was no blame attached to anyone. Came to the conclusion he must have dropped off to sleep with his hand on the whip as it was heaving in. Finished coaling at 2.00 p.m, having received 2,000 tons. 100 bags of coal were stacked on the upper deck.'

(McEwan's diary)
'At 6.00 p.m. we weighed and proceeded South. At 7.00 p.m.

we stopped while the burial service was held, the *Inflexible* being just off St. Vincent. It was a beautiful night.'

While the battlecruisers were coaling at St. Vincent, Sturdee received the latest Intelligence reports on the movements of von Spee, cabled to the Admiralty by the British Consul-General in Valparaiso. He had hired a number of small Chilean steamers to visit the harbours in the vicinity to search for the German cruisers or their supply ships. He was able to report that the German Squadron had been seen off Valparaiso Bay at dawn on 14 November. It wasn't a lot to go on. Sturdee had to find an enemy who might, at that very moment, be disappearing in any direction into the vast wastes of the Pacific or Atlantic. Worse; von Spee's Squadron might have split up. 'In a word,' wrote Barry Bingham, 'it was like looking for five needles in five bundles of hay, if the ships had dispersed and were acting independently.' Sturdee was faced with the prospect of a search that might take months before he cornered his quarry: if he were ever to find them at all. Two days out from St. Vincent the battlecruisers were fast approaching the Equator.

Saturday, 21 November
(Woodland's diary)
"Crossing the Line"
'Several heavy showers of rain in the fore-noon. At 10.00 a.m. went on deck to see Neptune (Lieutenant-Commander Dannreuther the Gunnery Officer) arrive in his royal car — a wooden throne on wheels — preceeded by the ship's band. Neptune was well got up as were his many attendants, particularly one in a crinoline skirt which did not reach his knees. Neptune was met by the Admiral, Commanders and Lieutenant Borrett presented him with an "Iron Cross". The Admiral addressed Neptune in a long speech on the war and the reasons for it — an excellent speech. Next came the initiation of those who had not yet crossed the line. Each man had his face lathered with soap, was then seated in a sort of chair overhanging a huge bath, while he was shaved with a big wooden razor, finally he was suddenly tipped over backwards into the bath to be ducked and smacked by

Neptune's attendants. I went through it early and got off very lightly. Some of the men had a bad time of it particularly those who tried to escape it. A game of hockey in the evening, then a bath. Afterwards 2nd Dog Watch in the decoding office with the bandmaster.'

Sunday, 22 November
(Woodland's diary)
'Forenoon Watch and First Watch in the decoding office, where I now take my regular Watches. The duties are to put into code wireless messages sent out and to decode wireless messages received. Divine Service on the poop under a big awning.'

(McEwan's diary)
'Beautiful morning, and we crossed the line at 4.15 a.m. As we crossed the line, I got a bottle of the sea water at the line, and another for Officer of the Watch.'

Monday, 23 November
(McEwan's diary)
'At dawn "Action" was sounded off, as we approached the Rocas Rocks. [It was rumoured that the armed merchant cruiser *Kronprinz Wilhelm* was using the rocks as a coaling base.] *Invincible* passed to the west and *Inflexible* to the east. It is the most extraordinary little island, there is only a lighthouse and a small house visible, the island itself being about a quarter of a mile long and half as broad, and the highest point is no more than fifteen feet above sea level. As nothing was found we proceeded south.'

Wednesday, 25 November
(Woodland's diary)
'A very hot day. Following received from Admiral Stoddart, Commanding 5th Cruiser Squadron: "Message dated 22nd November from Montevideo begins – *Scharnhorst, Gneisenau, Leipzig, Dresden, Nürnberg* last reported at Mas a Fuera Island [Chilean waters]. As I write there is much noise on deck, where they are getting out stores for the *Carnarvon* (Stoddart's flagship). We arrive at Abrolhos Rocks [70 miles off the Brazilian coast] tomorrow, where we

rendezvous with Stoddart's cruiser squadron and colliers with 37,000 tons of coal. Tonight the *Inflexible* was astern. She fired some "rocket shells" which looked fine as they burst high up in the sky.'

At dawn on the 26th the armoured cruiser *Kent*, which has sailed from Sierra Leone, joined up with the two battle-cruisers. The three ships arrived at the Abrolhos Rocks at 7.31 a.m. that morning. Waiting for them, riding at anchor, were nine colliers, an oiler and Stoddart's cruiser squadron consisting of the armoured cruisers *Carnarvon* and *Cornwall*, the light cruisers *Glasgow* and *Bristol* and the armed merchant cruiser *Orama*.

Fresh instructions from the Admiralty, working on the latest Intelligence that von Spee was still in Chilean waters, now directed Sturdee to . . . 'Proceed South with colliers and whole Squadron. Use Falkland Islands as main base for colliers. After coaling [at the Falklands] proceed to Chilean coast, avoid letting your large ships be seen in the Magellan Straits. Search the straits, inlets and channels taking colliers with you as necessary.'

Invincible's crew spent practically the whole day trans-ferring provisions to *Carnarvon* and engine room stores to *Bristol*, together with 54 bags of mail which they had brought out from England for the ships of Stoddart's squadron. Friday the 27th was spent coaling. From 7.00 a.m. until 9.45 that evening the men in *Invincible* toiled under a merciless, broiling sun to top up the depleted bunkers with 1,750 tons of coal. It is common for naval historians to criticize Sturdee's leisurely pace on the 7,000 mile journey to the South Atlantic [the battlecruisers averaged a mean speed of eleven knots], insinuating that the Admiral did not appreciate the need to close Chilean waters with all dispatch.

Geoffrey Bennett, in his book *Coronel and The Falklands*, states that the battlecruisers could have made a good sixteen–eighteen knots. The explanation for this seemingly slow pace was quite simply the fuel situation and the necessity of not over-taxing the engines on the long pull south. The ships did not have enough coal to proceed at a high rate of knots as they leap-frogged between the coaling bases (2,500 miles from Devonport to St. Vincent; 2,300 miles from St. Vincent to the Abrolhos Rocks; 2,200 miles from the Rocks to the Falklands) and the ships left St. Vincent with extra coal stacked on the deck. Sturdee also had to bear in mind that when he caught up with Graf von Spee's squadron of fast cruisers, if he were ever to do so, *Invincible* and *Inflexible* would need every ounce of power that their engines and boilers could provide to overtake Spee and bring him to battle. In the South Atlantic there were no dockyard facilities to overhaul the engines in case of excessive wear or breakdown and at full speed the battlecruisers only had a small margin of knots over the German armoured cruisers – a margin Sturdee could not afford to sacrifice on a mad dash across the Atlantic.

Sturdee led his reinforced squadron to sea at 10.00 a.m. on 28 November. *Orama* sailed later to escort the convoy of nine colliers and the oiler. Before sailing Sturdee had received a further Intelligence report that *Kronprinz Wilhelm* was operating off the River Plate. In the hope of catching the German raider he swept south down the trade route to the Falklands, with his squadron spread out on a fifty-one mile front.

Direction of Advance
(Speed 11 knots) ▼

Carnarvon 12 miles *Kent* 12 miles *Bristol*

12 miles

Glasgow 12 miles *Cornwall* 12 miles *Inflexible* 3 miles *Invincible*

Later that same day the armed merchant cruiser *Macedonia* joined the squadron, having coaled at Pernambuco in Brazil, after sailing from Sierra Leone.

On the afternoon of the 30th, Sturdee took advantage of the calm sea and excellent visibility for the battlecruisers to carry out some much needed gunnery practice [*Scharnhorst* and *Gneisenau* had reputations of being crack gunnery ships]. The practice was carried out at 12,000 yards, this being the range that Sturdee intended to engage von Spee's armoured cruisers. At this range, he believed, *Invincible*'s armour would be sufficient to resist the German 240-pound 8.2-inch armour-piercing shells. Of the 32 rounds (four from each gun) fired by *Invincible* at a target towed by *Inflexible*, only one hit was obtained; but the result, presumably because of near misses, was declared to be satisfactory. *Inflexible* faired a little better, scoring three hits on *Invincible*'s target out of 32 rounds.

Assistant Paymaster Woodland observed the firing from the after superstructure. 'The noise was tremendous,' he wrote, 'and I was glad to have cotton wool in my ears. When *Inflexible* fired at our target it was about half a minute after seeing the big flash of her guns that the shot hit the sea, the report being heard at the same time. The shells made a whistling noise like a big rocket. In spite of the firing, not much china, glass, etc., was broken.'

While *Invincible* was hauling in her target the wire hawser attached to the main derrick fouled and wound itself around the starboard outer propeller. Sturdee stopped the whole squadron [7.34 p.m.] while divers went down to unravel it. Their efforts were only partially successful, and not wishing to waste any more time, the squadron got under way again at 2.20 a.m., *Invincible* steaming with only three propellers.

As the squadron approached the southern latitudes the weather grew progressively colder, the sea turning from deep blue to a cold greenish-black colour. By Friday 4 December white uniforms were stowed away and blues became rig of the day. On the 5th, the ships were lost to sight of one another for most of the day in thick, damp fog. All watertight doors were closed in case of collision, and extra lookouts were posted.

Monday, 7 December
(Woodland's diary)
'I was up before seven to relieve the bandmaster in the decoding office for the last part of the Morning Watch. After

breakfast I went on deck and found that the Falkland Islands were in sight. We entered via a channel shaped like a dog's leg; on each side was rather bleak-looking rocky country with a few small bushes occasionally. I used my telescope continuously, and was lucky to spot a good many penguins, standing like sentinels on the shore.'

At 10.26 a.m., twenty-seven days and 7,000 miles since leaving Devonport, *Invincible* dropped anchor in Port William, the deep-water anchorage of the East Falkland Islands. [A narrow entrance, 300 yards wide, leads from Port William into the shallower waters of the inner anchorage of Port Stanley.] Within minutes of anchoring divers were sent down once more to tackle the urgent task of clearing the hawser from the fouled propeller. The work went on all day and through the night before the wire was finally unravelled.

While the rest of the squadron coaled (*Bristol* and *Glasgow* with their light draught in the inner harbour, and the armoured cruisers *Carnarvon*, *Cornwall* and *Kent* in Port William) the officers and midshipmen of *Invincible* and *Inflexible* enjoyed five hours' shore leave. 'I went ashore with Lieutenants John Le Seelleur (Royal Marines) and Alexander McMullen,' Wrote Woodland. 'As we passed round a bend into the inner harbour in the picket boat, we passed the *Canopus* [an old predreadnought battleship which had beached herself to act as a fort in case the German cruiser squadron attacked the Islands before Sturdee's arrival]. In Port Stanley were several whalers and old disused ships, amongst them the *Great Britain*. We met the clergyman in Stanley, who invited us to tea. He, Mr. Hobbey, late of St. Edmund's Hall, Oxford, is married with two children; the youngest about three years old, sat on my knee at tea and upset a cup of tea over me. We returned to *Invincible* by the 6.00 p.m. picket boat. After dinner McEwan and I tried fishing, but without success; it was awful cold on deck.'

That evening Sturdee called a conference of all the Captains on board the flagship. The latest Intelligence reports that German colliers had appeared at Montevideo and Dawson Island on the eastern side of the Magellan Straits, indicated that von Spee might be intending to round Cape Horn into the South Atlantic. In light of this Sturdee decided to sail on the following evening, 8 December, as soon as the battlecruisers had completed coaling, to round the Horn before von Spee and catch him as he came South down the Chilean coast. That at least was the theory.

7

Contact!
Providence Delivers up Von Spee

Tuesday, 8 December 1914 dawned very cold but bright and
clear with visibility at its maximum. At 4.30 a.m. the collier
Trelawney secured to the port side of *Invincible* and an hour
later all hands commenced coaling. By 7.30, when the ship's
company were piped to breakfast, 400 tons had been
embarked. At 8.00 a.m. the Officer of the Watch on the
bridge of the flagship was alerted by the report of a saluting
gun fired by *Glasgow* in the inner harbour; she then signalled
by lamp: 'A four-funnelled and a two-funnelled man-of-war
in sight from Sapper Hill steering northwards.'

Arthur Dyce Duckworth, a young Sub-Lieutenant on
Sturdee's staff, recalled how, while at breakfast in the
Wardroom (the third cup of coffee, toast and marmalade
stage had been reached), 'A black figure rushed in announcing excitedly that two men-of-war had been sighted on
the horizon to the southward. At first this was regarded as a
false alarm. We had heard too many rumours to pay much
attention to this one. However, the fact that two warships
were approaching the Islands from the direction in which the
enemy might possibly be expected sent one or two up to the
tops to verify matters for themselves. These confirmed the
previous report and it dawned on us that "there was
something doing" at last.'

Sturdee, who was shaving when he was informed of the
report by the Flag Lieutenant, calmly ordered the colliers to
be cast off and the whole squadron to raise steam for full
speed. At 8.30, with a further report that smoke from three
other ships was visible twenty miles to the southward, Action
was sounded off. There could be no doubt now, von Spee's
whole squadron was obligingly sailing straight towards them
and prospects of having to spend weeks or months searching
for the enemy were carried away on a chorus of cheering.

While the stokers and engine-room staff of *Invincible* were frantically engaged in the process of raising full steam and reassembling the boiler mountings which they had begun stripping down, *Canopus* opened fire on the two leading cruisers [9.19 a.m.] with her two forward 12-inch guns at a range of 11,000 yards. They were, in fact, *Gneisenau* and *Nürnberg*, scouting ahead of von Spee's squadron. Both shots fell short by a mile, but a shell from the second salvo of three guns at extreme elevation richochetted and hit *Gneisenau* [it was, in fact, a practice shell which had been loaded the previous night in preparation for a trial shoot). This caused the two cruisers to veer away eight points to the east.

It was nearly two hours after Sturdee had given the order to raise steam before Engineer Commander Weeks could report to Captain Beamish that the ship was ready to proceed. As *Invincible* started to move down harbour at 10.00 a.m., a cutter loaded with mutton and flour, left behind by *Inflexible*, drifted across her bows. Stopping for nothing the great ram bow of the battlecruiser sliced the boat in two throwing each portion contemptuously aside as the ship gathered speed. The squadron passed Seal Rock, which marked the end of the southern lay of the harbour, into open water after 10.30 a.m., in the order *Carnarvon*, *Inflexible*, *Invincible* and *Cornwall*. They were joined off Port William by *Kent* and *Glasgow* which had sailed earlier to report on the movements of the enemy. [*Bristol* was still in the inner anchorage trying to raise steam.]

'I was struck', wrote Sub-Lieutenant Duckworth, 'by the magnificent weather conditions and seizing my camera climbed up the mast into the Main Top. The air was biting cold as I and two Signalmen, who were stationed aloft as spare hands, stood and watched the enemy nineteen miles away to the south-west – five triangles of smoke on the horizon. It was a brilliant sunny day, visibility at its very maximum. And there they were, the squadron that we thought would have kept us hunting the seas for many weary months. They had been, it seemed, providentially delivered into our very hands. All hands not closed up at the guns, etc., were employed in cleaning as much of themselves and the ship of coal dust as could be possibly done. Now was the time to stow away anything of value and to put one's affairs in order as of course no one knew what might happen to any of us.'

Sub-Lieutenant Stewart's diary (he was in 'A' turret)
'*10.35 a.m.* 23 knots. Course S57W. Roughly calculating we should come into range of the enemy in about 2½ hours, i.e., about 1.00 p.m. *10.50 a.m.* Every lamp in the ship went out, owing to extra power being wrongly divided to the dynamo – no control communications in the turret. *11.00 a.m.* Communications corrected. Still no lights in turret, only auxiliary lighting.'

By 11.15 a.m. the squadron had become strung out, the slower armoured cruisers *Carnarvon* and *Cornwall* lagging behind by five miles. As the battlecruisers had gained quite considerably on the fleeing Germans, and Sturdee was quite confident that he could overtake them whenever he thought fit, he decided to reduce speed to nineteen knots to allow the slower ships to catch up. The enemy was now well in sight from the flagship, their funnels and bridges showing above the horizon. So confident was he that at 11.32 he signalled to the squadron: 'Ships' Companies have time for next meal.' 'Had a picnic lunch in the Wardroom,' Woodland wrote, 'tongue, bread butter and jam.'

The engine room artificers in *Invincible* had rigged a rope ladder in the air inlet leading up to the vent fans on the weather deck so that they could take it in turns to nip up on deck and see what was going on. Here they joined a crowd of others who, not wishing to miss the spectacle by taking a meal on the mess decks below, had grabbed chunks of bread and cold meat and come back up top.

By 12.20 the slower ships had fallen even further behind and Sturdee, not wanting to delay opening the action any longer, ordered the battlecruisers to increase to full speed. The enemy cruisers were ten miles off *Invincible*'s starboard bow, spread out line abreast on a two-mile front.

At full speed *Invincible* and *Inflexible* made an impressive sight to all who witnessed them. Ram bows foaming into the steely green sea, sterns leaving boiling wakes, five white 'battle' ensigns fluttering from the yards standing out in stark contrast to the thick black, oily smoke pouring from their funnels, the huge guns searching out the enemy at full elevation. *Inflexible* was steaming parallel to *Invincible* slightly on her port quarter. When 'Action' was again sounded off in *Invincible* at 12.30, clearing the deck of spectators as they dashed to their battle stations, the battlecruisers had worked up to twenty-six knots – one knot in excess of their designed speed.

The first shot of the battle was claimed by Captain Phillimore [known throughout the service as 'Fidgety Phill'] in *Inflexible*. He opened fire from 'A' turret with a two-gun salvo at 12.55, the guns on the stops to achieve the maximum range of 16,500 yards. Fire was directed at *Leipzig* which had fallen 3,000 yards astern of the German squadron. Two great fountains of water rose 200 feet out of the sea a thousand yards short of the target. Two minutes later [12.57] *Invincible* opened fire with a two-gun salvo from 'A' turret, but once again the shells fell short. It wasn't until 1.15 (according to Stewart), when the range was down to about 15,000 yards, that the battlecruisers managed to straddle *Leipzig*. She was almost lost to view among a forest of shell splashes. One shell from the left-hand gun of *Invincible*'s 'A' turret, falling close to her bows, drenched the cruiser in a deluge of cascading sea water. Five minutes later it was observed from the flagship that the German squadron was splitting up; *Leipzig, Dresden* and *Nürnberg* altering course to starboard, while *Scharnhorst* and *Gneisenau* turned east-north-east directly into the path of the oncoming battle-cruisers; 'turning like cornered animals steadying themselves for combat that might save their young'.

In accordance with Sturdee's battle instructions [issued at the Abrolhos Rocks] *Kent, Glasgow* and the lagging *Cornwall* took off after the fleeing light cruisers without waiting for a signal from *Invincible*. Determined to accept action with von Spee's armoured cruisers beyond the range of the German 8.2-inch guns (13,500 yards), but within range of his own big guns (16,500 yards), Sturdee immediately swung round seven points to port onto a parallel course with *Scharnhorst* and *Gneisenau*, 14,000 yards distant.

The scene was set for the very last naval action that would be fought in the old traditional broadside for broadside manner, without the complications of torpedoes, mines, submarines and aircraft. Lieutenant-Commander Smyth-Osborne, in command of *Invincible*'s 'P' turret, was confident that it would all be over within an hour. After all, the battlecruisers had a crushing superiority in broadside fire over the two armoured cruisers (combined weights of 10,200 pounds against 3,914 pounds). But it wasn't going to be that simple.

8

The Finest Hour
The Battle off the Falklands

As the two squadrons steadied onto a parallel course of east-north-east, they immediately opened fire on each other: *Invincible* engaging the *Scharnhorst*, *Inflexible* the *Gneisenau*. A light breeze blowing from the north-west put the two battlecruisers at a disadvantage as it carried the thick funnel smoke and the great clouds of cordite gas, belching from the gun muzzles, between them and the enemy. The only clear view of the German cruisers was obtained by the rangefinders in *Invincible*'s 'A' turret and by Lieutenant-Commander Dannreuther, *Invincible*'s Gunnery Officer, high up in the fore-top. The smoke almost completely blinded the gunners in the midships and stern turrets, while *Inflexible* suffered the dual disadvantages of her own smoke and that from *Invincible* blowing across her line of vision.

The first two salvoes fired by *Scharnhorst* fell short, but von Spee had turned towards the battlecruisers, and with the range rapidly diminishing to 12,000 yards, the third salvo straddled *Invincible*. 'Five columns of water simultaneously shot into the air all round the ship,' Duckworth recalled. 'At the noise of the approaching shells I involuntarily ducked my head!' Choking with the fumes that were slowly asphyxiating him [the main-top was situated directly abaft the third funnel], he struggled down the interior of the 'nearly red hot vertical leg of the tripod mast and retreated to the After Medical Distributing Station below decks to lend a hand with the Chaplain and Sick Berth staff. Here one could only hear and feel the shock and shudder of our gunfire and hope that some of the detonations were not enemy shells hitting us.' Apart from the dim glow of the auxiliary lighting, the ship was still in total darkness and would remain so for the whole of the engagement. Smyth-Osborne in 'P' turret [which was firing across the deck from the disengaged side] was dismayed to observe that 'we did not seem to be hitting the *Scharnhorst* at all'.

The gunfire of both battlecruisers was, in fact, very slow and inaccurate. This was due mainly to the excessive smoke and the forest of enemy shell splashes which kept spouting around the ships, at times entirely hiding von Spee's cruisers from view. Dannreuther [who, ironically enough, was a godson of the German composer Wagner] found that the stereoscopic rangefinders in the fore-top were rendered useless by the smoke, the extreme range and the vibration in the top caused by the high speed of the ship and the violent shaking of the mast whenever 'A' turret fired. Without the rangefinders he had to resort to the primitive use of binoculars to spot the fall of shot and estimate the range with the assistance of a 'spotter' using a telescope. To make matters worse he couldn't see the shots which fell 'over' the target as they were hidden by *Scharnhorst*'s smoke.

In 'Q' turret, which was manned entirely by Marines under the command of Major Robert Colquhoun, conditions were impossible. Not only could they see nothing except the enemy gun flashes through the enveloping clouds of smoke, but every time 'P' turret fired over them the gunlayers, trainers and sight-setters were deafened and dazed and had there heads banged against adjacent projections. So bad was it that their orders had to be shouted into their ears.

They weren't the only ones in trouble. At 1.42 p.m. the breach of the right-hand gun in 'A' turret jammed and it was thirty minutes before the gun could be brought back into action. 'Luckily', wrote Sub-Lieutenant Stewart, 'we drew off from the enemy about this time. Leveson [Lieutenant (E)] came into the turret to assist, and we managed to open the breech with crow bars. We had to put a new observation port in as the old one seized up. This caused some delay as a new port had to be fetched by one of the artificers from 'P' turret, where all the spares were stowed. Eventually, however, we got the gun working again. It continued to give us trouble, however, as we were constantly getting missfires.'

Well did *Scharnhorst* live up to her reputation as a crack gunnery ship for at 1.44 p.m. she hit *Invincible* with one of her 8.2-inch shells. It burst against the flagship's side armour and was felt as a severe tremor all over the ship. The shell failed to penetrate the armour and apart from tearing off the covering plate did no real damage. By this time the range had fallen to 12,000 yards so Sturdee, who was directing the battle from the director tower on the mast just below the fore-top, ordered a turn to port to open it out again beyond the range of the German gunners. At the same time he reduced speed to twenty-two knots to lessen the effects of the funnel smoke. For the next fifteen minutes the two squadrons gradually drew apart until the battlecruisers were beyond the maximum range of the German guns. At 2.00 p.m. fire was checked and the ear-splitting, mind-numbing din of battle was replaced by an unnatural silence.

During this first thirty minutes of the action the two battlecruisers had, between them, fired a total of 210 rounds of 12-inch ammunition. Out of these, *Inflexible* had scored three *certain* hits on *Gneisenau* while *Invincible* could only claim one *probable* hit on *Scharnhorst*. At this rate the battlecruisers would empty their magazines of ammunition without sinking the enemy. Even when they did score a hit the damage so far, due to the defective bursting capabilities of the British shells, had been superficial. The only damage to *Gneisenau*, worth mentioning, was an 8.2-inch gun put temporarily out of action. Dannreuther had been surprised to see how many shells had failed to explode as they should have done when hitting the water.

Shortly after the battlecruisers ceased fire, von Spee attempted to escape by turning sharply away to the south. Over the horizon clouds were gathering. If he could only hold off the battlecruisers until they reached those clouds, which promised poor visibility and perhaps mist, there would still be a chance of escape into the night which would begin to fall in four or five hours' time.

Because of the blinding smoke, it took a few minutes for those in *Invincible* to realize what was happening, but immediately Sturdee became aware of von Spee's south-easterly turn, he swung the battlecruisers round and gave chase at twenty-four knots. The pursuit lasted a full forty minutes before the range was finally reduced to 15,000 yards and the battlecruisers, turning slightly to port to bring their broadsides to bear, re-commenced their cannonade. If von Spee continued his run to the south he would play Sturdee's game by being unable to reply to the British fire because of the shorter range of his guns. He had no choice, therefore, but to turn back on to an east-north-easterly course at 2.53 p.m. and place his ships in the path of the oncoming battlecruisers. Sturdee parried with a turn to port and once more the two squadrons faced each other on a parallel course – broadside to broadside.

Although the battlecruisers were still suffering from the adverse effects of the funnel smoke they both began to score hits on their respective adversaries. By 3.03 p.m. the range had diminished to 11,000 yards: a range at which the Germans could bring their secondary batteries of 5.9-inch guns into action. For the next fifteen minutes *Invincible* was repeatedly hit by both 8.2-inch and 5.9-inch shells.

One 8.2-inch armour-piercing shell burst inside the starboard strut of the foremast, which not only tore away ten feet of the strut and riddled the forefunnel with shrapnel, but also blew open the manhole-cover leading to the fore-top. 'The blast', Dannreuther reported, 'was somewhat severe and knocked everyone down in the top and wrecked the rate transmitter. It did not do much material harm but to be knocked down is disconcerting to the Control Officer and entails missing the fall of a salvo.'

Duckworth was still in the After Medical Distributing Centre together with the Fleet Surgeon (Walter Bearblock), the Padre (Arthur Moreton) and several Sick Berth Stewards sitting on the stretchers. 'We felt several hits,' he wrote, 'and suddenly the atmosphere became thick with smoke. The fan which was running hard keeping the compartment ventilated was pouring in smoke. We quickly raised up the hatch above to the mess decks to get out and soon were all stumbling about in a thick fog of dust, steam and smoke. The hoses were running full [hoses were left running on the upper deck in action to lessen the danger of fires] and the mess was indescribable. The Mess tables and stools were down and all the gear belonging to each Mess was lying about in pools of water. With a loud report one of the upper bunker lids flew off while a cold in-rush of air from the blast of 'Q' turret momentarily knocked everybody flat. The fire was soon located in the Sick Bay on the port side, but it was some time before it was got under. [*An 8.2-inch shell had struck the deck near 'X' turret, plunged down through two decks before bursting in the Sick Bay – which was empty of personnel.*]

About this time too the ship's canteen began blazing and, do what we could, it could not be got at properly and ultimately burnt itself out completely. Our party now collected its gear and set off to join up with the Fore Distributing Station. I got on to the Main deck once more and made my way forward. In the Wardroom I found all four bulkheads riddled like a nutmeg grater, an enormous hole in the outboard side with a large hole immediately below it on to the deck below and another on to the upper deck through which daylight was streaming. In the middle of what was left of the Wardroom was a heap of rubbish and wreckage – consisting of the long Wardroom table and the meal that had been laid out at lunch time. I passed hurriedly on through the Admiral's dining cabin to the Midshipmen's flat. Here another gash in the deck above and sundry twisted bits of iron shewed the entrance of another shell. Down once more and I was making my way to the forward shell room. Once inside the cylindrical casing I felt more or less secure. Here indeed were signs of activity. Parties of men tending the loading trays, rolling the 12-inch "projes" into them and inscribing in chalk tender messages to the recipients thereof.'

One of the engine-room artificers, in a letter written home after the battle, recounts how he 'went up top for a fanny of water. As I was returning a shell burst in the canteen [this was an 8.2-inch shell which entered through the upper deck abreast 'X' turret on the starboard side]. As you can guess I did not waste much time getting down below. About five minutes later a stoker came down with an armful of fags and tins of pineapple. The stokers were all smoking cigars and yaffling (eating) chocolate, pineapple, etc., looted from the wrecked canteen. Every now and again we nipped up to see

Above: The launch of *Invincible* from the Elswick yard on the Tyne, 13 April 1907. (NPL)

Below: *Invincible*, 1909. Commissioning pennant flying from foremast. (IWM)
Bottom: *Invincible* in 1910. (MOD)

Right: *Invincible*, 1912. (IWM)

Right: *Invincible, circa* 1912/13. (IWM)

Above: *Indomitable*, 1909. Ammunitioning ship with 850lb, 12-inch shells. (NMM)
Below: *Indomitable*, coaling ship. 'P' and 'Q' turrets have been elevated and trained inboard. View taken from the base of the after shelter deck looking forward. (IWM)

Top right: *Invincible* at the 1911 Spithead review. (NMM)
Bottom right: Portsmouth harbour, 1911. Nearest the camera is the battlecruiser *Indefatigable* and beyond her *Invincible* and two armoured cruisers. (IWM)

Left: The Falkland Islands, Sunday, 8 December 1914. Taken by Sub-Lieutenant Arthur Dyce Duckworth from *Invincible*'s maintop. *Inflexible* and *Cornwall* are raising steam in Port William, prior to getting under way. (IWM)

Bottom left: Photograph taken from foretop of *Carnarvon* at approximately 10.45 a.m., of *Invincible* chasing von Spee's Squadron. (IWM)

Top right: The smoke from *Gneisenau* (left) and *Nürnberg* faintly visible 15 miles distant from *Invincible*. Photograph taken by Duckworth. (IWM)

Centre right: *Invincible* has gained on the fleeing *Gneisenau* and *Nürnberg*. On the left of the picture is *Glasgow*, 3 miles distant from *Invincible*. (Duckworth, IWM)

Bottom right: Smoke from the five German cruisers, hull down on the horizon. *Leipzig* is far out on the starboard wing. (Duckworth, IWM)

Top left: Photograph taken from *Glasgow* of *Invincible* making 22 knots during the chase. Note excessive funnel smoke which was to make life hellish for the gunners during the battle. (IWM)

Centre left: Photograph taken from *Kent* at 1.00 a.m., during the chase. (IWM)

Bottom left: Photograph by Duckworth of

Inflexible opening fire from 'A' turret on *Leipzig*, 12.55 p.m. (IWM)

Above: Vice-Admiral F. C. Doveton-Sturdee (1859–1925). This photograph was taken on the battleship *Hercules* in 1915. (IWM)

Below: Photograph by Duckworth of *Inflexible*, picking up survivors from *Gneisenau*. (IWM)

Left: *Invincible* in dry dock at Gibraltar, January 1915, undergoing repairs to damage sustained during the Falklands battle. Note the barrel of the 4in gun (arrowed) which was cut in half by a plunging shell. (Photograph by Midshipman Allan McEwan, IWM)

Right: *Invincible* in dry dock at Gibraltar. The shell hole in the side of the hull is abreast Seamen's Mess on the Main Deck. The deadlight under the gangway, through which the officer is looking, opens from the Wardroom on to the upper deck. (Photograph by Midshipman Allan McEwan, IWM)

Below: Two battlecruisers of the *Invincible* class in the foreground, and two of the *Indefatigable* class in the background, berthed below the Forth Bridge, 1915. (IWM)

Left: Rear-Admiral, The Ho[norable]
Horace Lambert Alexander
Hood (1870–1916). Hood
hoisted his flag in *Invincibl[e]*
on 27 May 1915, and
commanded the 3rd Battle
Cruiser Squadron until the
destruction of *Invincible* at
Jutland. Hood's widow
launched the battlecruiser
Hood, the keel of the ship
being laid down on the very
day that he lost his life, 31
May 1916. (IWM)

Below: An aerial view of
Inflexible. Showing the dec[k]
layout of this class of
battlecruisers. (IWM)

Opposite page, top left:
Commander Hubert Edwar[d]
Dannreuther (1880–1977),
who served as *Invincible*'s
Gunnery Officer from 1912
until the loss of the ship at
Jutland. Photograph taken i[n]
1915. (HHD)

Opposite page, top right: A
post-Jutland photograph of
Lieutenant R. Ross Stewart
with an American naval
officer. Ross Stewart was
serving as Rear-Admiral
Hood's Flag Lieutenant at th[e]
time of Jutland, but was
fortunately on leave from the
ship when the *Invincible* set
sail for the last time on 30
May 1916. (Captain R. Ross
Stewart)

Opposite page, bottom left:
Midshipman Allan McEwan
in 1914. (Mrs. S. M. McEwa[n]

Opposite page, bottom righ[t]:
Paymaster Arthur Dyce
Duckworth, R.N., 1914. (Mr[s]
Grace Duckworth)

Left: The 3rd Battle Cruiser
Squadron during the Battle
Jutland. (IWM)
Centre left: 6.34 p.m., 31 M
1916. *Invincible* blows up
after being hit by a salvo fro
the German battlecruiser
Derfflinger. (IWM)
Below: Lat 57° 2′ 40″ N, Lo
6° 7′ 15″ E. The wreck of
Invincible about 25 minute
after the explosion. The
destroyer *Badger*
approaching the target whi
four of the six survivors wer
using as a raft. In the
background are the
battleships *Superb* and
Canada of the 4th Battle
Squadron. This photograph
was taken at 7.00 p.m. from
the battleship *Benbow.*
(IWM)

what was going on. There was a crowd of stokers on the mess deck looking through a shot hole about three feet in diameter while some were scouting for fires and others smoking or hunting for curios, broken watches, bits of shell, etc.'

Not all of the German shells exploded. One 8.2-inch armour-piercing shell cut off the muzzle of one of the forward 4-inch guns on the starboard side, descended through two decks and, passing through a bulkhead screen, finally came to rest in a cupboard in the Admiral's storeroom, port side. Nicely burnished, this shell became a valued trophy on display in the Wardroom. A 5.9-inch shell plunged through the forecastle deck, entered the Chaplain's cabin, wrecking the reverend gentleman's wardrobe, tore through the bulkhead into the Fleet Paymaster's cabin where it hurled the gold sovereigns from the money-chest out onto the main deck, before passing harmlessly out through the port side of the ship.

Paymaster Gordon Franklyn describes his impressions of this stage of the action: 'On board the noise was simply deafening as round after round left the muzzles of the 12-inch guns. Up in the control position from time to time could be heard the cry of "six coming!" or "five coming!", as flashes of fire on the enemy ships announced that a salvo had been fired at us. Seconds passed, and then came the whirr and shriek of the shells and the final huge "Whoomph, Whoomph" as they rained down in the sea just short or just over. Some found their billet with a resulting explosion.' Allan McEwan's impression (he was assisting with the dead reckoning calculations in the forward conning tower) was that 'it was most weird hearing the shells whistle over us. When they hit the whole ship vibrated and staggered. Then you heard the splinters flying like hundreds of kettles and pans being thrown about.'

By now the results of the battlecruisers' gunnery had become visible. A blaze was seen forward in *Scharnhorst* and by 3.12 p.m. her fire had perceptibly slackened. Her steering gear was also damaged for she suddenly sheered outwards to starboard on a south-easterly course which opened the range by a mile. *Gneisenau*, conforming to *Scharnhorst*'s turn away, was also suffering from *Inflexible*'s fire. She had been hit below the waterline. Two boiler rooms were flooded, reducing her speed to eighteen knots and she was listing to port to such a degree that her 5.9-inch guns could no longer be elevated enough to reach *Inflexible*. Barry Bingham in 'A' turret found that 'At first it was difficult to differentiate between the flash of the enemy's guns and one's own hits, but observation soon enlightened me on the fact that when you really strike home on a ship you see a little red glow, or in the case of lyddite a cloud of yellow smoke.'

By 3.15 p.m. the interference from the smoke, which was playing havoc with the gunlayers and spotters, became so intolerable that Sturdee led the battlecruisers round to port, navigating a complete circle from which they emerged at 3.30 p.m. on a south-westerly course with *Inflexible* leading. This placed the battlecruisers on the windward side of the German ships and for the first time they had a clear view of their target. During the turn two of *Scharnhorst*'s 8.2-inch shells struck *Invincible*'s quarterdeck. These wrecked the seamen's 'heads' and the prison cells and holed a fire main which flooded the electric store and paint shop. As they came out of the turn a 5.9-inch shell exploded on the front plate of 'A' turret, between the two guns, which rocked the whole turret. 'If the shell had struck thirty inches higher,' wrote Bingham, 'it would have sent the sighting hood, rangefinder operator and myself to glory.' As it was, it only dented the turret armour but it holed the gun aprons with the result that every time the guns fired the personnel in the turret were subject to the blast and the choking effects of the sickly cordite fumes which the aprons were designed to eliminate. As Sturdee assumed his south-westerly course, von Spee parried by turning a half-circle to starboard, once again attempting to cross the bows of the battlecruisers. With the handicapping smoke now considerably lessened and the guns trained to port for the first time in the action, *Invincible*'s gunnery began to have a telling effect. 'I had "Q" turret firing across the deck,' wrote Smyth-Osborne in 'P' turret. 'They practically put my turret out of action, their blast deafening and dazing my gunlayers, spotters and trainers. In fact making all those in the gun house partly damned stupid. In the excitement the Marines in "Q" were firing on some dangerous bearings.'

Scharnhorst was almost hidden by the smoke from bursting shells and internal fires. She was down three feet below the waterline, her third funnel had been shot away and according to Gordon Franklyn: 'Her upper works were a shambles of torn and twisted steel and iron, and through the holes in her side, even at the great distance we were from her (12,000 yards) could be seen the dull-red glows as the flames gradually gained mastery between decks.' Dannreuther recalled that: 'She was being torn apart and was blazing and it seemed impossible that anyone could still be alive.' Despite the terrible damage being wreaked upon her, von Spee's flagship managed to keep up a slow but steady succession of salvoes, scoring a hit on *Invincible* which nearly proved fatal. An 8.2-inch shell struck the ship below the side armour under 'P' turret. It tore a hole in the side plating, four feet by two feet, which flooded number five coal bunker (the sea washing out most of the coal) and broke up (without exploding) against the thinly armoured bulkhead separating the bunker from the magazine. This magazine, which lay practically across the whole width of the ship, fed both 'P' and 'Q' turrets. If the shell had exploded and red-hot fragments had penetrated the thin internal armour surrounding the magazine, there is every possibility that the cordite would have ignited and the ship would have been blown in half.

At 4.00 p.m. *Scharnhorst*'s guns fell silent. *Invincible*'s 12-inch shells had reduced her to a wreck. Her funnels were lying at all angles, she was ablaze forward and aft, and her bows were so low in the sea that the waves were washing over the forecastle. Listing heavily to port, swathed in escaping steam, she drifted helplessly out of line towards her tormentors, her flag still bravely flying. At this point the armoured cruiser *Carnarvon*, which had been cutting corners to catch up with the battlecruisers, arrived on the scene. She got in on the kill by opening fire on the dying ship with her 7.5-inch guns at a range of 11,000 yards. But *Scharnhorst* was already settling. She heeled gradually to port, her bows dipping deeper into the steely green, icy sea. The stern rose into the air and, with her screws still turning, she made her death plunge into the deep amidst a great hissing geyser of steam and smoke. With her she took von Spee and 850 officers and men. Not a soul survived. Bingham records that when he relayed the news of the sinking to the men in the working chamber, handing-room and magazine below 'A' turret 'the men responded with loud cheering, which mingled with cheers which rose from every part of the *Invincible*.'

The fire of the two battlecruisers and *Carnarvon* was now directed at *Gneisenau*. Passing astern of the sinking flagship, firing as she went, she maintained a south-westerly course towards the rain clouds which were drawing nearer. But with her speed reduced to eighteen knots, there could be only one ending. Still suffering intermittently from the effects of the funnel smoke, *Invincible* and *Inflexible* turned two complete circles within the next half-hour to clear themselves of the blinding pollution while maintaining a position off the starboard quarter of *Gneisenau* at ranges between 9,000 and 12,000 yards.

Despite being outnumbered three to one, the German cruiser continued to give a good account of herself, fighting it out alone for an incredible one hour and forty-five minutes. Sub-Lieutenant Stewart in 'A' turret made detailed notes of this period of the battle:

4.15 p.m.   About to alter course to starboard. Guns to train as we go round. [This was the first circle navigated to get clear of the smoke.]

4.23 p.m.   Target on bearing green 90, 10,200 yards. *Gneisenau* seems to be suffering badly.

4.25 p.m.   *Gneisenau* directing her fire at *Invincible*.

4.27 p.m.   Shots burst over *Invincible*.

4.29 p.m.   *Invincible* hit. Range 9,600 yards. 'X' turret reports only armour-piercing shells left.

4.33 p.m.   Target on bearing red 40.

4.38 p.m.   *Invincible* hit. Only Lyddite shells left in 'A' turret magazine.

4.42 p.m.   *Gneisenau* badly hit.

4.43 p.m. *Invincible* hit forward. [This hit was by an 8.2-inch shell which exploded on the armour belt at the water-line. The plates were fractured and bent inwards, resulting in the flooding of a bow compartment.]

4.45 p.m. Range 9,250 yards. Our shots falling short and to the left of target.

4.49 p.m. Speed 15 knots. 'A' turret running short of ammunition. Only ten or twelve full charges left. Our shots falling short.

4.57 p.m. Enemy bearing red 60–12,500 yards.

5.08 p.m. Forefunnel of *Gneisenau* shot away by 'A' turret.

5.15 p.m. *Invincible* hit forward. An effective hit on *Gneisenau* between 3rd and 4th funnels. [The hit on *Invincible* was made by an 8.2-inch shell which burst on the armour belt to no effect.]

5.27 p.m. Bridge of *Gneisenau* brought down.

5.30 p.m. *Gneisenau* listing to port – appears stopped.

5.34 p.m. Checked fire – closing enemy.

5.35 p.m. Enemy on bearing red 30. *Carnarvon* and *Inflexible* closing us. Range 10,150 yards.

5.45 p.m. 'Q' and 'X' turret fired.

5.48 p.m. Speed 12 knots.

5.49 p.m. *Gneisenau* practically a wreck. One turret firing.

5.50 p.m. *Gneisenau* stopped, but occasionally firing her gun. Listing to starboard – appears to be sinking. Speed 10 knots.

5.53 p.m. Cease firing.

5.55 p.m. All turrets standing by to open fire at any moment.

6.00 p.m. *Gneisenau* flat on her side in the water.

6.02 p.m. *Gneisenau* sank.

Just before the end, visibility suddenly reduced considerably as a drizzling rain set in. By the time the last shots were fired at her *Gneisenau* had become a very faint target on which to range. She had finally reached the clouds and promise of bad weather which could have saved her – two hours too late. Listing heavily to starboard, steam and smoke pouring from her

shell-riven hull, she heeled over onto her beam ends at
6.00 p.m. and hung in this position for a few minutes before
slipping under the waves, leaving about 300 of her complement of 850 struggling in the chill Antarctic water. 'The men
were fearfully excited,' wrote C. F. Laborde, the Captain's
clerk in *Inflexible*, 'and they rushed forward on to the fo'c's'le
shouting and cheering, but the Captain ordered the "alert" to
be sounded and everybody stood to attention in silence as she
sank.' As if to mark her grave, steam and smoke rose from the
surface of the sea and hung in a thin cloud over the position.
Duckworth describes what happened next.

'It was just after 6.00, a drizzling rain had set in with a
biting cold southerly wind. The sea had a steady swell. Away
ahead of us on the dull leaden water appeared a small pale-
green patch of water containing a clustering mass of
humanity. The wind brought the most dismal and awful cries
from the survivors of the sunken ship. The *Invincible* and
Inflexible steamed slowly into the midst of this mass,
lowering boats and ropes. Both ships stopped, slowly heaving
on the swell, funnels without a scrap of paint and in many
cases perforated through and through, no canvas round the
fore bridge, twisted guard rails in the superstructure, riddled
bulkheads everywhere and a four-inch gun barrel rolling to
and fro on the upper deck. Cutters were now laden with
survivors. All around the ship there floated bodies, some on
hammocks, some on spars, others struggling by themselves,
others drowning slowly before one's very eyes before any
boat could reach them. Most were so numbed that they could
not hold on to anything and were absolutely helpless. Many
were terribly wounded and mangled, others seemed very
much alive under the circumstances. On all sides one saw all
our men hauling up the half-frozen bodies up the side and
carrying them down to the Admiral's cabin.'

'There was one poor fellow bobbing along the side of the
ship,' Stewart recalled, 'and Lieutenant Hugh Begbie went in
after him, having put a bowline around himself. He secured
another bowline around the man and we hauled him up. This
was done in many cases. It was an awful job getting them up
over the ship's side, especially over the net shelf.' Clement

Woodland, who had been stationed in 'A' turret magazine throughout the action says, 'The water was so cold that it killed many poor fellows before we could reach them. I noticed a live torpedo floating near us [fired by *Gneisenau* just before she sank]. This was fired at by some of our Marines with rifles, in an attempt to explode it. When most of those we could reach had been picked up, I went below and did my best to bring round some of the rescued. I worked hard on one poor fellow: he was just alive, but in spite of my efforts he finally died. I got hold of a bottle of brandy and forced it into the mouth of each man I possibly could.'

Invincible picked up seven officers and 104 men, twenty of whom were found to be dead or died shortly afterwards of their wounds and exposure. *Inflexible* picked up eight officers and 55 men and *Carnarvon* two officers and 31 men. 'Below in the Admiral's cabin,' wrote Duckworth, 'those we had picked up were all laid out and classified as dead or living – a gruesome but necessary procedure. Duffel coats, blankets and hot soup were handed out. The doctors were up to their neck in work. The Wardroom anteroom and Gunroom were also utilized as shelters for the survivors, the officers being separated from the men.'

It was all over. The battlecruisers had vindicated themselves in the very role that Fisher had envisaged for them. But it hadn't been quite the all one-sided battle of annihilation of which he believed them capable. After the battle Fisher castigated Sturdee's tactics as 'dilatory and theatrical – à la William Terriss' [an actor, noted for his breezy style]. But Sturdee had quite rightly kept the range extreme. It would have made no sense at all to have fought it out at close range and thereby risked greater damage to the battlecruisers than they in fact received. 'Why should he have taken chances with all the trump cards in his hand?' It had taken 4½ hours and about 1,150 12-inch shells to sink the two armoured cruisers. The total expenditure of ammunition by the battlecruisers was 1,174 (*Invincible* 513, *Inflexible* 661), but approximately 24 shells had been fired at *Leipzig* before the main action began. Added to this great weight of shell (nearly one million pounds) was the 85 rounds of 7.5-inch and 60 rounds of 6-inch ammunition fired by *Carnarvon* (mostly at *Gneisenau*) which brings the grand total of shells fired at von Spee's armoured cruisers to 1,295.

Out of this massive expenditure the number of hits scored is estimated at 74 (40 on *Scharnhorst* and 34 on *Gneisenau*), but this might be an overestimate, because Midshipman Freiherr Grote, a survivor from *Gneisenau*, who kept a detailed account of the action in a notebook, records only 23 hits on *Gneisenau*. The difficulty in sinking the two armoured cruisers was ascribed to the poor shooting of the battle-cruisers due to the extreme range at which the action was fought; the interference from the gun and excessive funnel smoke; and the rugged watertight construction of *Scharnhorst* and *Gneisenau*. Matters weren't helped by the numerous minor faults which occurred in the newly installed hydraulic machinery in *Invincible*'s gun turrets. In his official report on the action (PRO. Adm. 137/304, folio 224) Sturdee made reference to the fact that: 'Ever since I hoisted my flag in the *Invincible* there have been continual partial failures in the hydraulic machinery . . . fortunately nothing serious occurred during the action, but the general fittings cannot be considered entirely satisfactory.' Apart from the jamming and continual misfiring of the right-hand gun in 'A' turret, the left-hand gun had to be taken out of action towards the end of the battle. The air-blast pipe, which sucked away the fumes, was broken by the recoil of the gun with the result that when the gun was fired the turret filled with suffocating cordite smoke. And if that were not enough, the piping in the turret leaked to such an extent that Stewart described it as 'tropical rain'. In 'Q' turret the breech of the left-hand gun proved difficult to open and, like the personnel in 'A' turret, the Marine gunners had to 'assist' it with crowbars.

Captain Beamish's report contains two pages cataloguing a whole host of mechanical problems that occurred in the gun turrets. Rammers failed; gun-cages transporting the shells and cordite to the guns jammed; along with numerous failings of a nature too technical to be appreciated by the layman. All this smudged over the most important lessons – the defective bursting qualities of the British shells (only

72

Dannreuther suspected that something was wrong) and the need for more intensive target practice at long ranges. The only time that Dannreuther, as Gunnery Officer in *Invincible*, had fired at ranges in excess of 6,000 yards was during the practice on the way south to the Falkland Islands, and he had joined *Invincible* as 'Gunnery Jack' in 1912!

Invincible, whose fore part had always been visible for spotting and ranging on, was hit a total of twenty-two times (twelve 8.2-inch, six 5.9-inch and four unidentifiable). Apart from the two flooded bow compartments and the flooded coal bunker alongside 'P' turret magazine (which gave her a 15° list to port), the damage was superficial and in no way impaired her fighting qualities. There were eleven hits on the deck (seven of these on the forecastle), one on the after conning tower, two on the unarmoured part of the starboard side, four on the armour belt, one below the waterline, one on 'A' turret, one on the starboard bower anchor and one on the starboard strut of the foremast. Added to this was the self-inflicted damage of distorted beams and broken planking caused by 'P' and 'Q' turrets firing across the deck. Incredibly, not one of the ship's company was killed and there were only two minor casualties: Commander Townsend received a badly bruised foot caused by a bag-rack falling on him when a shell burst near-by, and a stoker cut his arm while fighting a fire.

Because *Inflexible* had been hidden for long periods in the smoke from the flagship, she received only three hits. The worst damage was caused by a shell bursting against the top of the main derrick; splinters from which killed an able seaman and wounded three others who were sheltering behind 'X' turret.

Radio messages received from the other ships of the British squadron had kept Sturdee informed of their progress in bringing to action the remainder of the German cruisers. It was known that *Bristol* and *Macedonia* had sunk the German colliers *Baden* and *St. Isabel*, and that *Cornwall* and *Glasgow* were in action with *Leipzig* (which they sank at 8.35 p.m.), but nothing had been heard from the old armoured cruiser *Kent*. *Invincible* was unable to raise her on the radio and, as

Nürnberg and *Dresden* were unaccounted for, Sturdee feared the worst and at 7.30 p.m. he set off with *Inflexible* to the south-west making for *Kent*'s last known position. *Carnarvon* was sent north to escort *Orama* and the convoy of colliers which were still plodding along at eight knots on their way south to the Falkland Islands.

At 8.00 p.m. Sturdee dispatched a signal to the Admiralty announcing his victory. 'I shall never forget that telegram being sent,' Duckworth wrote. 'The Secretary (Cyril Johnson), myself, Captain Beamish, the Flag-Lieutenant (Reginald Blake) and the W/T Officer were all in the coding office wording the momentous message. Admiral Sturdee came in and having agreed on its phrasing, ordered it to be sent at once to Port Stanley, from there to be sent 1,000 miles again by W/T to Montevideo and from there by land-wire direct to their Lordships in the Admiralty.'

At midnight, with the battlecruisers under way for Cape Horn and into thickening weather, one of the engine-room artificers coming off watch went on deck for a breath of fresh air. 'There were about ten bodies', he wrote home, 'naked and stacked up like so many hammocks. Some had terrible burns, others had half their face or shoulder torn away. I turned in and slept like a top.'

9

Recall
The Victors Return

The 9th of December was spent in the fruitless search for *Kent* and *Dresden* and *Nürnberg*: pausing only to commit the bodies of the dead German sailors to the deep with full military honours.

Invincible and *Inflexible* were navigating through thick fog towards Staten Island at the eastern tip of Cape Horn, when a message from *Macedonia* (3.00 p.m.) announced that she had sighted *Kent*. She was making for Port Stanley, having sunk *Nürnberg* at 7.27 p.m. on the previous evening. She had been unable to report her movements because her wireless had been damaged in the action. This still left *Dresden* to be accounted for, but as the battlecruisers were running short of coal, Sturdee had to abandon the search and return to the Falklands. Sweeping north they sighted Jason Island off the north-west coast of the West Falklands at 5.00 p.m. on the 10th, and arrived in Port William at 6.30 a.m. on the following morning.

Friday, 11 December 1914
(Woodland's diary)
'Got up at 5.30 a.m., as the bandmaster wanted me to help with a wireless message. I found we were close to Port Stanley. I went up on deck as we entered into the harbour. *Cornwall* was in, with a bad list, and also the *Kent* with many signs of having been in action. In the morning I helped the Padre with the claims for personal belongings of the officers destroyed during the action.'

(McEwan's diary)
'It was a bitterly cold and windy day. Divers were sent down to investigate the amount of damage to the port side where we were hit below 'P' turret. A hole six feet by seven feet was discovered so we had to set about patching it up temporarily.

75

We gave ourselves a list of 15 degrees to starboard for the work to be put in hand. The day was spent in getting up empty cordite cases on to the upper deck and transferring them to a supply ship. In the afternoon a service was held in the church at Port Stanley for the funeral of the seven men killed in *Kent*. I attended very wet and cold, for we had got soaked through in the picket boat on the way. In the evening the Captain of *Inflexible* with the Commander of *Gneisenau* (Hans Pochhammer) came on board to dine with the Admiral.'

In the early hours of Sunday the 13th, Sturdee received a report from Captain Milward, the British Consul at Punta Arenas in the Magellan Straits, that *Dresden* had arrived in the port on the afternoon of the 12th and was coaling. Sturdee immediately ordered *Inflexible*, *Glasgow* and *Bristol* (the three fastest ships) to sail for Punta Arenas. After coaling, *Carnarvon* and *Cornwall* sailed (4.00 p.m.) to work down the eastern seaboard in case *Dresden* eluded Phillimore's three ships and doubled back into the South Atlantic.

It was Sturdee's intention to join the search with *Invincible* as soon as the flooded coal bunker had been pumped dry and the hole below the waterline had been sufficiently patched to make her seaworthy. But this was vetoed by the Admiralty who ordered Sturdee to return home with *Invincible*: the battlecruisers could not be spared for the tracking down a solitary enemy light cruiser. *Inflexible* was withdrawn from the chase on 19 December and diverted to the Dardanelles. As for *Dresden*: she was eventually brought to bay at Mas a Fuera three months later (14 March 1915) by *Glasgow, Kent* and *Orama*. She scuttled herself to avoid capture.

Invincible remained at Port William for another three days, repairing the damage and redistributing the remaining 257 shells in equal number among the magazines. (At the end of the action 'A' turret had only twelve shells left, 'X' 29, 'P' 112 and 'Q' 104. This was a shortfall of 110 if the full load of 880 shells – 110 rounds per gun – had been carried).

Tuesday, 15 December
(McEwan's diary)
'Coaling commenced at 3.30 a.m., with 2,200 tons to come

in. Everybody seemed in great form and I'm sure that if we'd had good winches we could have put up a very good average. Our best hour was 166 tons, and we averaged 130 tons an hour. With the usual breaks for meals, coaling went on until 11.00 p.m. I was fortunate to have a break from lunch till tea, when I was Midshipman of the barge which took the Admiral on a trip to see the penguins.'

(Woodland's diary)
'Called at 3.00 a.m., dressed, had some cocoa and bread and butter, then commenced coaling. I started by helping to tip the coal from the sacks down the shutes, and continued till my wrists were feeling weak. I personally finished coaling at 8.00 p.m. when I cleaned up. My eyes were quite bloodshot from the coal dust. Just after coaling commenced a young man on the collier got his leg caught in a winch and it was torn off. During the morning the *Kent* left harbour [to join in the search for *Dresden*] and she cheered us as she passed.'

Wednesday, 16 December
(McEwan's diary)
'The upper deck was stacked with coal. Before lunch we unmoored and rode to a single anchor. At 2.00 p.m. we weighed and proceeded out of harbour, setting course for Montevideo.'

Friday, 18 December
(McEwan's diary)
'Dawn came about 3.15, later than the last week or so. It is considerably warmer; fresh wind and slight swell and quite fine. The hands were employed in painting the superstructure all day. Most of our holes from splinters have been patched up.'

Sunday, 20 December
(McEwan's diary)
'Anchored off Montevideo early in the morning [5.55 a.m. Seven miles off shore]. Very fine morning but the wind increased before the evening when severe rain and a thunderstorm occurred. The lightning was extraordinarily vivid. The *Invincible* looked very fine indeed with her new

coat of paint and white decks. At 8.00 a.m. when the colours were hoisted we fired a salute of 21 guns.'

(Woodland's diary)
'At 2.00 p.m. some of us took advantage of a small tug, which brought out a newspaper reporter, to go on shore. The journey took about an hour. The tug was very small and the sea was quite rough, in fact at times we seemed as though we would capsize! The reporter and one of our company were very seasick. Luckily I felt perfectly well and I stood by the man at the wheel and thoroughly enjoyed it.'

(McEwan's diary)
'We drove in taxis from the landing-stage to a hall where there was a reception in honour of *Invincible*'s visit. On entering the hall the Admiral was given a warm reception, being received by the English, French and Belgian Ministers. Soon after six we returned to the tug and were back on board by 7.00 p.m. for dinner. We weighed and proceeded at 8.15 p.m.'

While *Invincible* was anchored in the River Plate the Wireless Officer visited the wireless station at Ceritos with the purpose of having a number of telegrams sent to the Admiralty. [All messages received and sent from the Falklands to London had to be passed through this station.] The wireless operator at the station warned him that the German battlecruisers *Seydlitz, Moltke* and *Von der Tann* were in wireless telegraphy with Montevideo. Because of the limited range of wireless telegraphy in those days, these battlecruisers had to be in the Atlantic. 'Our situation was not an easy one,' wrote Dannreuther. 'We were by ourselves in a somewhat damaged condition with very little ammunition on board (32 rounds per gun) and were hardly a match for three German battlecruisers. A cable was sent to the Admiralty asking for news of these German ships and reporting that until we received more definite information we were proceeding south again to the Falkland Islands to concentrate there with the *Inflexible*.'

The Admiralty replied within two hours with the information that 'For certain the ships you mention were in the

North Sea on 16 December.' Turning north-east, *Invincible* once more headed for home. 'The origin of this rumour,' Dannreuther believes, 'was probably as follows. On the way out we boarded as many steamers as possible and it was very noticeable how nearly every ship whether English or foreign, endeavoured to escape, firmly believing, till the boarding officer arrived on board, that we were German battlecruisers. Probably the merchant ships were deceived by the light colour of our paint, which was like the German colour and much lighter than the colour they had been accustomed to see in English men-of-war. These rumours, once started, were spread as much as possible by the large number of wireless stations in South America that were heavily subsidised and practically run by Germans with a view, no doubt, of frightening our trade. The call signs of these three battle-cruisers were often made and we picked them up on one or two subsequent occasions. So it turned out we were haunted by our own shadows.'

Retracing the coaling station leap-frog of the outward bound journey, *Invincible* took on coal (1,800 tons) at the Abrolhos Rocks on the 26th and at St. Vincent which she reached on 4 January 1915.

Monday, 4 January 1915
(McEwan's diary)
'Anchored at St. Vincent (6.26 a.m.). We received our first mails since leaving England – 156 bags – from the Battleship *Vengeance*. At 8.00 a.m. the collier *Indiana* was secured alongside the starboard side. She had 1/8th of our ammunition on top of the coal. The cordite came alongside the port side in lighters.'

Tuesday, 5 January
(McEwan's diary)
'Started coaling at about 7.00 a.m., the second collier coming alongside soon after 6.45. We had 2,160 tons to come in. We did better than usual, averaging 176 tons an hour.'

Invincible left St. Vincent on the afternoon of the 6th bound for Gibraltar where she would be dry-docked for repairs to the damage she had received in the Falklands battle.

Friday, 8 January
(McEwan's diary)

'Heavy northerly swell made us roll a little during the night. A strong easterly wind was blowing and the masts, bridge and superstructure were covered with a thin layer of brown sand blown right out from the Sahara Desert. After tea a very fine fight was held on the quarterdeck between two ordinary seamen, who'd had a difference between them in the forenoon. After 23 rounds, owing to failing light, the contest was declared a draw.'

Monday, 11 January
(McEwans diary)

'We entered the Straits of Gibraltar soon after 7.00 a.m. It was a perfect morning, but cold; the sea was absolutely calm. Steaming at 19½ knots we entered the harbour at 9.00 a.m. On our way in we passed the Light Cruisers *Inconstant* and *Penelope*, who cheered us. In the harbour we passed the Armed Merchantman *Calgarian*, and the Battleship *Caesar* who is stationed out here as a Gunnery Training Ship. We cleared lower deck and cheered ship. We secured alongside the South Mole, going into dry dock at 5.00 p.m.'

Invincible remained at Gibraltar for a month while the damage was repaired and an extra fifteen feet of casing was added to the fore-funnel to alleviate the interference from the funnel smoke to the bridge. [The fore-funnels of *Inflexible* and *Indomitable* had been heightened before the war.]

Sturdee and his staff left the ship on 28 January, homeward bound on the P. & O. liner *India*, to raise his flag in the battleship *Hercules* as Commander of the 4th Battle Squadron of the Grand Fleet. 'It was a sad parting,' Woodland wrote in his diary, 'for the Admiral was so much liked by the whole ship's company. He shook hands with each officer and as he left the ship, officers and men gave him three good cheers. It was quite obvious that the men loved him and did not want to lose him. He is a fine sailor and a perfect gentleman.' For what Admiral Sir Richard Webb described as 'The greatest sea victory the British Navy has known since Trafalgar', Sturdee was awarded a baronetcy in the 1916

New Year's Honours List and a grant of £10,000. With Sturdee went Sub-Lieutenant Duckworth and Barry Bingham, who had been promoted to Commander and given command of a destroyer. 'As we stepped over the *Invincible*'s gangway and walked down the dockside to the picket boat that was to take us out to the *India*,' wrote Bingham, 'the whole of the ship's company mustered on deck, manned ship, and led by Captain Beamish gave the Admiral three rousing cheers. For my part the leave-takings and these ringing cheers produced a reaction of the greatest depression. It meant leaving a good ship in which I had been intensely happy, and above all, a wardroom of the best lot of mess-mates I have every served with – where harmony and accord prevailed amongst one and all.'

On 9 February Clement Woodland also left the ship, being transferred to the old battleship *Albion* which was bound for the Dardanelles. 'My life on board HMS *Invincible* is now over,' he wrote in his last diary entry. 'I have had a splendid three months in her and have learnt to love her, so that it is a hard blow to have to leave.'

10

Hood Takes Command

Repairs completed, *Invincible* sailed from Gibraltar at 2.00 p.m. on a very wet and windy Saturday, 13 February, bound for Scapa Flow. It proved to be a very unpleasant passage. On Tuesday she steamed into heavy rain and a south-westerly gale which gave her a 24° roll, a huge following sea continually swamping the quarterdeck.

She arrived at Scapa at 7.00 on the 19th, anchoring among the great concourse of battleships, cruisers and destroyers of the Grand Fleet. The next eleven days were spent in gunnery exercises, the programme being constantly dogged by rain squalls, bitterly cold wind and driving snow storms. The reason for the trial was to test the newly installed 'Director Firing System'. Vickers' engineers had been carried on board since her commissioning in August to assist with the complicated installation of the system's heavy electric cables. Unfortunately they had been unable to complete the work before the Falklands battle, as it would undoubtedly have resulted in a greater degree of accuracy. 'Director Firing' meant that all the 12-inch guns could be aimed and fired simultaneously from a control position fitted on the foremast just below the fore-top. One man [Dannreuther in *Invincible*'s case] used a master sight – a single telescopic sight electrically connected to the sights of each gun. He aimed the ship's broadside and fired it by pressing a single key. This method helped considerably to improve accuracy. Most of the gunnery was carried out in the exercise area inside the Flow (to the east of the fleet anchorage) with the sub-calibre method. This consisted of fixing a 3-pound or 6-pound gun inside the bore of the 12-inch guns so that the sub-calibre could be fired at a target while exercising the training of the turrets and the main armament control. Only once during the eleven days was full-charge firing carried out. 'We proceeded

82

out of Scapa Flow and anchored the target 1,150 yards off Switha,' Midshipman McEwan recorded in his diary. 'Invincible fired thirty-two 12-inch shells, at a range of 12,000 yards. The splashes were 270 feet high.' The results of the exercise are not recorded, but it did become apparent that four of her 12-inch guns had become 'worn' during the Falklands battle and would have to be changed. In particular the inner tube of the left-hand gun of 'A' turret (which had fired 109 rounds in the action) was found to be protruding half-an-inch outwards from the muzzle.

On the afternoon of Wednesday, 3 March Invincible in company with Indefatigable, which had also been undergoing gunnery trials at Scapa, sailed for Rosyth to join the newly constituted Battlecruiser Fleet. Invincible was now under the command of Captain Arthur Lindsey Cay who had relieved Beamish on 23 February.

The new Battlecruiser Fleet under Beatty's command had been brought into being as a direct result of an event that had occurred on the day Invincible set sail for home from the Falklands. On 16 December 1914, the German battlecruisers Seydlitz, Moltke, Von der Tann and Derfflinger and the powerful armoured cruiser Blücher carried out a tip-and-run raid on the east coast of England. Operating in two groups they shelled Scarborough, Hartlepool and Whitby, killing 122 and wounding 443 of the inhabitants. To counter the possibility of a repetition [and in response to the criticism of the Press that the whole fleet was too far north] the Admiralty decided (20 Dec) to shift the battlecruiser squadron from their base at Cromarty further south to Rosyth where they would be better placed to intercept a raiding force.

The constitution of the new 'Fleet', which was formulated on 21 February 1915, formed the ten battlecruisers into three squadrons. Each squadron had a light cruiser squadron attached to it for scouting purposes, and was to be screened by the sixteen destroyers of the 13th Flotilla. The organization of the squadrons was:

1st Battlecruiser Squadron
Lion Fleet flagship (Vice-Admiral Sir David Beatty)
Princess Royal (Rear-Admiral Brock) Queen Mary, Tiger

2nd Battlecruiser Squadron
Australia (Rear-Admiral Pakenham), *New Zealand, Indefatigable*

3rd Battlecruiser Squadron
Invincible (to be flagship), *Inflexible, Indomitable*

Due to the dispositions of the various battlecruisers this organization was not completed until the summer. *Indefatigable* and *Inflexible* did not arrive from the Mediterranean until late March and 27 June respectively. *Invincible* remained in the River Forth (except for five brief excursions into the North Sea with the battlecruiser fleet) until 25 April. At 4.00 p.m. on the 25th, screened by three destroyers, she proceeded south to her birthplace on the Tyne to have the four 'worn' 12-inch guns replaced at Walkers Yard, Newcastle. While the work was under way the ship's company was given their first home leave since joining the ship at the outbreak of war eight months previously. Four days was granted to each watch in turn. During this period [she remained on the Tyne until the 12 May], Midshipman Allan McEwan, who had kept his detailed diary every day since joining *Invincible*, left the ship. He transferred to the Royal Naval Air Service, and served as an airship pilot until 1919, logging 2,400 hours of airship flying and attaining the temporary rank of Captain, Royal Air Force, in addition to his substantive rank as Lieutenant, RN.

At the end of May 1915 the appointment to command the 3rd Battlecruiser Squadron, which had remained vacant since the inauguration of the Battlecruiser fleet, was filled by Rear-Admiral, The Honourable, Horace Lambert Alexander Hood, who hoisted his flag in *Invincible* at 9.50 a.m. on the bright, clear morning of Thursday, 27th May. 'Bertie Hood', as he was affectionately known in the Service, was born into a distinguished naval family on 2 October 1870. He was the third son of the 4th Viscount Hood, a lineal descendant of Admiral Samuel Hood (1724–1816), a name famous in British naval history.

Possessed of a shy, almost child-like simplicity of manner, he was none the less regarded as an officer of exceptional merit who would have gone to the very top if he had not been killed at Jutland. 'He had an intense sense of duty and moral courage of the highest order,' is Admiral Richmond's assessment. 'He took responsibility readily, and never hesitated to follow a course of action that might be unpopular or prejudicial to his personal interests. To this courage he joined a love of active pursuits and an acute and hearty sense of humour.' In 1910, at the age of 40, he married Ellen Touzalin, an American from Massachusetts, whom he met while serving as Naval Attaché in Washington in 1908; they had two sons.

After commanding the Naval College at Osborne (1910–13) he was promoted to Rear-Admiral (May 1913) and in June 1914 became the Naval Secretary to the First Lord (Churchill). He held this post until October 1914, when he was given command of the Dover Patrol; a force of elderly destroyers used to patrol the Straits. It appears that neither Churchill nor Fisher had much confidence in him because he was bombarded with 'prodding' signals and instructions from the Admiralty, finally being relieved of his command in April 1915 and transferred to a force of elderly cruisers working the North Atlantic patrol out of Queenstown. Although Churchill informed Hood that his supersession had nothing to do with Admiralty dissatisfaction with the way he had handled his command, Hood clearly thought otherwise because he protested about his treatment to Fisher but with no effect. He also wrote to Beatty who replied on 15 May saying that he thought he had 'been treated abominably' and offering him the vacant command of the 3rd Battlecruiser Squadron. Hood at once accepted, receiving his official appointment on 22 May.

Almost one year to the day of Hood hoisting his flag in *Invincible*, both Rear-Admiral and ship would meet their end together. Ironically, he was lost on the very day that the keel of the battlecruiser *Hood* (named after his illustrious sea-going family) was laid down.

11

The Year of Waiting
Home Waters, May 1915
to May 1916

May 1915 to May 1916, the last year of *Invincible*'s existence, [and that of Hood and the majority of her 61 officers and 965 men], was to be one of boredom, frustration and disappointment. This was a result of the defensive strategy employed from the very beginning of the war by both the British and German battle fleets. Jellicoe would not accept battle in the southern waters of the North Sea because of the fear of mines and submarines. He aimed to fight a fleet action in the waters north of latitude 56°. Conversely, the High Seas Fleet was just as terrified of mines and submarines and would not subject itself to similar disadvantages by fighting in the northern latitudes. The result was like a game of chess in which both players refuse to risk their chessmen by moving over the centre of the board.

For the officers and men of *Invincible* the months of waiting for the day of reckoning with the German fleet, with little activity beyond the usual monotonous, unproductive sweeps into the North Sea, periodic target practices, tactical exercises and incessant coaling, grew increasingly tiresome. The battlecruiser fleet was normally kept at four hours' notice for steam, which allowed for only short excursions ashore. To alleviate boredom and sustain morale, sport was encouraged and inter-ship rivalry quickly developed. At Rosyth, eight football pitches were laid down for the men, and for the officers a rugby pitch and two hockey pitches. The Marines were landed once a week for a compulsory route march. A 'wet' canteen was constructed on the recreation ground, to sell beer, stout, tea, coffee, mineral waters and pastries. It was opened for the afternoon libertymen between 1.30 and 4.30 p.m. Beer and stout could only be purchased by tickets: a 1½-pence ticket purchased a half-pint, the maximum allowed being two tickets per man.

There were occasional cases of desertion among *Invincible*'s lower deck and the tedium even affected Hood who, in a letter to his mother-in-law, Alice Touzalin, declared: 'When the war ends I shall settle down on shore and spend the rest of my life bringing up my children and gardening.' On hoisting his flag in *Invincible* he had moved his family to North Queensferry House alongside the battlecruiser base, whereby he was able to 'see a lot of my family. I lunch ashore, play golf and motor; but every day I get up not knowing whether we may not in 2 or 3 hours be in an engagement in the North Sea: it is a funny life.' According to Assistant Paymaster Gordon Franklyn, the periodic sweeps at sea did nothing to alleviate the tedium: 'at sea, our thoughts centre on a single subject – the enemy – and it is only natural that we seem to lose absolutely the true perspective of ordinary things. Cooped up as closely as we are, trivialities of at all an irksome nature are apt to become enormities, and outside one's work petty peculiarities of a messmate – at first not even noticed, then whimsically tolerated – now after a few days' bad weather seem absolutely abhorrent. For instance, one gets to the stage of considering it a personal insult that one's *vis-à-vis* splutters whilst drinking his tea! At times one takes a feverish delight in welcoming additional discomforts (which must be bad!), and a green sea down the Ward-room skylight, resulting in the mess for an hour or two being an absolute snipe marsh, seems to be the best tonic going for a general "mouldy" atmosphere.'

On Monday, 19 July 1915, Midshipman Alexander Scrimgeour joined the ship, having transferred from the armed merchant cruiser *Alsatian*. Through his diary and letters he was to chronical life aboard *Invincible* for the last eleven months of her service. '*Invincible* is absolutely different from any previous ship I have served in,' he wrote to his mother at the end of July, 'but it does not take long to settle down. I am still senior Midshipman, as the seven Snotties (Midshipmen) already here are all junior. As far as I can judge, we seem to have a very nice lot of officers. *Invincible* is the flagship of Rear-Admiral Hon. Horace L. A. Hood, C.B., M.V.O., D.S.O., R.N. as he with all the etceteras. As I dare say you remember, he was Captain (before his promotion) at Osborne, when I was there, for one year. He is directly descended from the famous Admiral Hood of Nelson's time, one of the three brothers, all Admirals, Lord Hood, Lord Bridport, and Sir Alexander Hood; a nephew, son of a fourth brother, Sir Samuel Hood, was also a well-known Admiral. Thus they are about the most famous of all naval families. The member in question is reputed to be about the most brilliant of the younger school of flag officers, and is simply bulging with brains, so he is a pretty distinguished man to serve under. I expect you remember my telling you when at Osborne, that he is thoroughly Americanised, talking with a distinct Yankee twang, and having married an American Millionairess. With the single exception of Beatty, he was promoted to flag rank at an earlier age than any other Captain in the last fifty years. Yesterday I went to tea with Mrs Hood and family; they have a house on shore near our base, with a tennis-court and some excellent strawberry beds. As there are two A1 daughters of 17 and 19 (by Ellen's first marriage), you can bet their hospitality is full appreciated. There are also two little boys of six and two. Most of the married officers have imported their wives and families up here, as we are by no means constantly at sea. Leave is very limited, as of course we are always ready to sail at very short notice, and we can only get on shore for a few hours in the afternoon when not too busy. The Beattys are very much in evidence here; they have taken a huge place on shore in the vicinity [Aberdour House], and the anchorage simply stinks of Lady Beatty's hospital ship, yachts, motorboats, etc.'

The year dragged on:

12–14 June 1915. P.Z. exercises with battlecruiser fleet and Grand Fleet to the North of the Shetland Islands. (P.Z., were tactical exercises, so called after the flag signal P.Z. which indicated that they were to be performed). Night firing with 4-inch guns [eight rounds per gun] and 12-inch gunnery practice [four rounds per gun] at a target towed by a collier at a range of 12,000 yards.

10 and 11 September 1915. 1st and 3rd Battlecruiser Squadrons supported a minelaying operation in the Heligoland Bight. No enemy vessels sighted.

23–28 September 1915. 3rd Battlecruiser Squadron, at Scapa, sub-calibre firing inside the Flow. Rain and strong northerly winds throughout the period.

29 September 1915. Invincible left Scapa at noon for Belfast to dock and refit, screened by the destroyers *Shark* and *Acasta*. Ship's company granted leave in two watches (48 hours each watch).

6 October 1915. Invincible undocked Belfast at 8.00 p.m. and sailed for Rosyth screened by the destroyers *Achates* and *Fortune*.

(Scrimgeour's diary)
'Rejoined *Invincible*, after leave, in Harland & Wolff's yard, Belfast at 9.00 a.m. All the dockyard work complete, and we are ready to sail. In the afternoon I went ashore and rambled around the dockyard, a perfect beehive of shipbuilding industry. Went over the monitor *Earl of Peterborough* and the gigantic White Star liner *Britannic*. Proceeded out of dock at 8.00 a.m., met an escort of two destroyers off Carrickfergus, and proceeded out of Belfast Lough, shaping course for Mull of Cantyre [sic] and Oversay.

Thursday, 7 October. I kept the morning watch, proceeded past Dubh Artach, Skerryvore, Barra Head, and through the Minch and round Cape Wrath. General Quarters in the forenoon. Everything pretty efficient in 'A' turret. The men hardly seem to have got much benefit from their leave. Forty-eight hours, considering the time they spend travelling and the long periods elapsing between their leave, is too short, as they have a very monotonous time otherwise.

Friday, 8 October. Arrived at the Forth at 8.00 a.m., anchored, and the collier *Camerata* came alongside immediately. A terrific "coalship", 1,400 tons, the biggest we have had, lasting until 4.00 p.m. Very tedious and hard work. Coaling is an evil no landsman has experienced. The foc's'l'e hold swept the board; I worked the in-board winch fairly satisfactorily, and de Lisle [Lieutenant] seemed very pleased as he stood me two sherries afterwards. Felt really done in at the end. The Commander does not encourage the men as much as he should.'

14 October 1915. Invincible led the 3rd Battlecruiser Squadron, screened by six destroyers, from Rosyth for Cromarty, via the Noss Head channel, for full-calibre gunnery practice.

(Scrimgeour's diary)
'Went up north of the Moray Firth mine-field, then ran down the Sutherlandshire coast and into the Cromarty Firth, anchoring between Cromarty and Invergordon at 4.00 p.m. Commenced coaling at seven and took in 420 tons from the collier *Kilsyth*: finished at 10.30 p.m. Very uncomfortable and tricky work coaling in the dark.

Saturday, 16 October. Weighed at 8.00 a.m. and went out to do full-charge heavy gunfiring in the Moray Firth. A film of the firing was taken from the light cruiser *Active*. We fired with the *Indomitable*, and the *Inflexible* fired with the *Vanguard* of the 1st Battle Squadron. All the loading went off swimmingly in "A" turret, much to the delight of de Lisle and myself. All glass in the ship broken by the firing and all small fittings dislodged. A gorgeous day. Left the Firth and proceeded into the North Sea. In the evening we ran into a thick fog.

Sunday, 17 October. Entered the Firth of Forth and anchored in our usual billet at 9.00 a.m. Coaled ship from the collier *Slav*, 800 tons in very nearly record time. Everything went swimmingly except that [Midshipman] Campbell got jammed by a hoist of empties and twisted his hip very badly. A fine day, but the nip of winter returning in the air.

Saturday, 6 November.
'We unmoored, weighed and proceeded to sea at noon in company with *Lion*, 1st Battlecruiser Squadron, and rest of 3rd Battlecruiser Squadron. Carried out sub-calibre firing off

May Island, then parted company with *Lion* and 1st B.C.S. and proceeded east for the Skagerrak. The Germans have set a line of armed trawlers across to prevent the ingress of our submarines into the Baltic. Two light cruisers are going over to strafe the trawlers, and we are supporting them in case of eventualities. I kept the first dog-watch below in the engine-room and boiler-rooms with [Lieutenant 'E'] Alexander Macmullen. The boilers are in such excellent trim that it is very hard to keep the steam down to the necessary pressure.

Sunday, 7 November.
Kept the middle watch down below with old Bull [Artificer Engineer], who was in a very surly mood. Very hot. At 8.00 a.m. we rejoined the *Lion* and 1st B.C.S. and proceeded east until noon, then ran down the Danish coast for an hour before altering course for Rosyth. The result of the stunt has not been divulged. A nasty sea in the evening and we rolled heavily. The starboard torpedo boom-heads came adrift and made enough clanking noise to drive anyone off their head, banging against the ship's side just outside the gun-room.

Monday, 8 November.
Entered the Forth and anchored at 8.45 a.m. Started to coal immediately. Coming into harbour, one of the light cruisers rammed and sank a collier in the middle of the fairway. Finished coaling at 2.00 p.m., having taken in 850 tons.'

From 28 November to 2 December the battlecruiser fleet was at sea for P.Z. exercises and gunnery practice.

(Scrimgeour's diary)
Sunday, 28 November.
'At 11.00 a.m. we went to short notice, raised steam, and at 5.00 p.m. proceeded to sea in company with the rest of the Battle Cruiser Fleet.'

Monday, 29th.
We (3rd B.C.S.) represented the German battlecruisers, and the 1st and 2nd B.C.S's represented our Battle Cruiser Fleet. We approached the Norwegian Coast and tried to slip up north unobserved, and escape into the Atlantic, but they scotched us; rather a dull affair. Full speed all forenoon

without undue forcing; we averaged 25 knots and touched 26½ – much ado down in the engine and boiler rooms. Old Weekes, the Engineer-Commander, the only one not to be flurried. Mogg [Engineer-Lieutenant] sent me requesting the old boy to come down to the starboard engine-room at once, as the vacuum was dangerously high. The dear old chap insisted on my squeezing into the engine-room lift with him; he stopped it half-way down, and suggested that this was an ideal place for kissing the girls, and also recounted how he told this to Admiral Milne when the latter was inspecting the ship, the Admiral answering: 'Go on, go on, Engineer-Commander, I'm not a damned girl.' Sub-calibre firing at 10.00 a.m. Everything in a hopeless muddle in "A" turret; de Lisle in a philosophical mood; Petty Officer Bailey, the director trainer, is a useless ullage. During the "dogs" the sea got up badly, and we began to roll and pitch like Old Harry, and the weather got worse all night. The whole Fleet proceeded north-west at 18 knots between the Shetlands and the Norwegian Coast.

Tuesday, 30th.
The weather still very bad; all the galley-fires put out, and the atmosphere in the gun-room rotten, as we were battened down. No cooked food going.

Wednesday, 1 December.
The weather moderated a good bit after day-break, although a big swell remained. Carried out 4-inch gun firing in the forenoon; being off watch, I went up in the foretop to watch the firing. After an hour's P.Z. exercise we formed in line-ahead in the following order: *Invincible, Inflexible, Indomitable, Lion, Princess Royal, Queen Mary, Tiger, Australia, New Zealand, Indefatigable,* and carried out firing with main armament. To me our show seemed execrable. Firing finished, we re-formed into Squadrons and proceeded for Rosyth, hoping to make the Forth River early tomorrow.'

The results of the gunnery exercises that had been carried out since May 1915 were what Beatty termed as 'terribly disappointing', and in some cases 'deplorable'. The gunnery efficiency of *Invincible* he declared to be 'good sometimes', while only *Queen Mary*, *Princess Royal* and *Inflexible*'s performance could be described as 'good'. Beatty hoped to make good these deficiencies by putting to sea once a fortnight for more practice firings, but this was not to be, partly because of a shortage of practice projectiles issued to the fleet. In fact, between May 1915 and March 1916 *Invincible* only fired her 12-inch guns on four separate occasions (four rounds per gun on each occasion), and carried out 10 sub-calibre practices. The range was never in excess of 12,000 yards. As *Invincible*'s lack of adequate practice was representative of the whole battlecruiser fleet, it is no wonder that they were outgunned at Jutland by the far more gunnery-efficient German battlecruisers. [Even before the war it was known that the Germans were carrying out regular gunnery practices in Kiel Bay at ranges as high as 14,000 yards.]

Wednesday, 8 December 1915, the first anniversary of the Falklands battle, found *Invincible* at anchor in the River Forth. Sturdee wrote to Hood: 'I should be very much obliged if you will have conveyed to Commander Townsend and the officers and men of your flagship *Invincible* my good wishes on the anniversary of our action off the Falklands, and my renewed thanks for their successful efforts on that occasion. May I wish you and all the *Invincible*'s continued success and good luck.'

'Anniversary of the victory of the Falklands,' wrote Scrimgeour, 'so the ship's company piped down all day and did no work, and most of the officers landed in the afternoon. We lit up (the boilers) all night owing to the high wind, so as to prepare to shift billet if necessary. All the Falkland veterans went over to celebrate in *Inflexible*; on their return we had them in the gun-room and did great execution in the cocktail line, everybody very cheery. A ship's company concert in the afternoon, which, I believe, was very good. At about 5.00 p.m., after dark, and in the middle of the concert an urgent signal arrived from the Rosyth signal station from Sub-Lieutenant Cobb in the first picket boat, stating that he had been rammed by a mud barge at the entrance to the dockyard and was in sinking condition. Much commotion caused. Lieutenant Murray, who was officer of the watch and was in the gun-room, rushed out in chase of an elusive boatswain's mate; the Commander bawled orders from the poop, and in record time got away the second picket boat to assist the first. The second returned two hours later with the crew of the first and all the details. Cobb appears to have acted in the most excellent manner, and in spite of the sleepy inefficiency of the dockyard authorities, managed to arouse the King's Harbour Master and get the boat alongside and hoisted by the big crane on the quay just before she sank. The accident occurred owing to the mud barge being very low in the water at the end of a long tow without lights. The accident did not prevent a rousing evening in the Ward-room, where all gun-room officers and warrants were guests of the Ward-room, in addition to Captain Beamish, who was the Flag-Captain, and Commander Barry Bingham, another "old" *Invincible*.'

The battlecruiser fleet remained at anchor in the Forth throughout December. Christmas Day, 1915 fell on a Saturday; for Scrimgeour and the majority of the ship's company, it was to be the last they would ever know. 'A very mouldy day to start off,' wrote Scrimgeour, 'owing to the foggy weather we have had of late. We raised steam, in case the Bosche try any games in the fog, so there was no leave. In the forenoon, headed by Hood, we all went round the mess decks, which were wonderfully well decorated, as was the whole ship. The usual ship's company funny parties. The day dragged wearily on; at 3.30 in the afternoon the Ward-room challenged us to a cutter race, and some lunatics accepted, pressed a crew and got badly beaten by two lengths. Mrs Hood presented us (the midshipmen) with a plum pudding and a Xmas tree. We dined at 7.30, and things began to look up a bit; eventually we had an A1 dinner and heaps of everything to drink, and we all got very biffed and sang and shouted until midnight, when we rushed howling on deck, and about 12.30 reached the Warrant Officers' Mess, where we joined in another sing-song, finally going to bed at 2.30.'

The first quarter of 1916 proved to be as frustrating and unproductive as the previous six months. During February

Invincible, and the rest of her squadron, carried out sub-calibre firing at Scapa, and one full-calibre shoot in the Moray Firth (four rounds per gun at ranges between 11,000 and 13,000 yards). In March (25th and 26th) she was in the company of the battlecruiser fleet, which spent 27 hours cruising in the vicinity of the Horn Reefs through gales and heavy snowstorms, to support a seaplane attack on the Zeppelin base at Hoyer (on the Schleswig coast). The German battlecruisers and two squadrons of battleships did actually put to sea on this occasion [the night of 25th/26th] but did not advance beyond Sylt, sixty miles south of the British battlecruisers, before turning back.

April proved more promising. At 7.00 p.m. on 24 April the battlecruiser fleet was ordered to raise steam and proceed to sea. Through intercepted German signals the Admiralty had learned that the High Seas Fleet had sailed from the Jade at noon, and were steering for the east coast of England with the object of bombarding Great Yarmouth. The battlecruisers sailed at 10.50 p.m.: 1st B.C.S. *Lion, Princess Royal, Queen Mary* and *Tiger*; 3rd B.C.S. *Invincible, Inflexible, Indomitable* and *Indefatigable* (temporarily attached, *Australia* and *New Zealand* were in dock undergoing repairs after having collided with each other). By midnight they were ploughing south at twenty knots into the teeth of a gale and heavy seas. The whole of the Grand Fleet was following, 165 miles astern, having sailed from Scapa at eleven. Hopes were running high, there seemed every chance of cutting off the Germans' retreat and bringing them to action.

The gale raged all night, damaging the screening destroyers, and making it difficult for *Invincible* and her squadron, rolling and pitching into the head sea, to keep up with the larger battlecruisers of the 1st Squadron. At 11.45 a.m., when action was sounded off, the battlecruisers were steaming at *Invincible*'s best speed of 25 knots. They were hoping to cut off the four German battlecruisers which had shelled Lowestoft and Great Yarmouth (4.10 a.m. and 4.42 a.m. respectively) and were now falling back on the German battle fleet which had steamed as far south as the open waters west of Terschelling (seventy miles from the British coast) in support. Unknown to Beatty the German raiding force had already crossed ahead of him (by a mere fifty miles) and were on the way home. At 12.30 p.m., with nothing in sight and all hopes of cutting off the enemy vanishing, the battlecruisers turned north and made their way disconsolately home. At 11.07 p.m. that night, when the battlecruisers were about sixty miles due east of Farne Island and steaming through thick fog, the patrol yacht *Goissa* rammed *Invincible*'s starboard quarter. The *Goissa*'s bows were broken off and remained stuck in *Invincible*'s stoved-in hull. Four able seamen in *Goissa* were killed and *Invincible*'s speed was reduced to twelve knots through flooding. The collision bulkhead of *Goissa* held, and she was eventually towed into the Tyne by a trawler. Pulling out of line and proceeding independently, *Invincible* limped back to Rosyth, where she arrived on the foggy morning of the 26th. A floating crane lifted *Goissa*'s bow section clear of *Invincible*, and at 9.00 a.m. on the following morning she docked for repairs. The extent of the damage can be gauged by the fact that she remained in dry dock until 22 May. The dockyard superintendent signalled the Admiralty [26 April]: 'To effect repairs to *Invincible* shortest possible time working day and night, necessary that following additional dockyard workmen be sent from southern yards for three to four weeks' temporary service at once. 100 shipwrights with four charge men. 48 riveters. 30 drillers with tools. Two charge men for riveters and drillers, and four supervision foreman and two inspector shipwrights.'

Hood transferred his flag temporarily to *Inflexible*, while the docking of the flagship gave the ship's company the unexpected bonus of home leave and the last chance to see their families: the sands of time were running out.

12

Disaster at Jutland

'They went into battle foreseeing probable loss, and they lost.'

Invincible undocked from Rosyth on the morning of 22 May 1916 and anchored once more among the battlecruiser fleet in the River Forth. Hood struck his flag in *Inflexible*, transferred to *Invincible* and, at 5.00 p.m. that afternoon, led his squadron to Scapa for nine days of gunnery practice. In case of emergency the 3rd B.C.S's place was filled by the 5th Battle Squadron, which arrived just before Hood departed. The 5th B.S. consisted of the fastest and most powerful battleships in the Grand Fleet: *Barham* (flag of Rear-Admiral Evan-Thomas), *Warspite, Valiant, Malaya* and *Queen Elizabeth*, the latter docking at Rosyth for a refit.

On 30 May, after eight days of sub-calibre firing and torpedo practice, *Invincible* led her two consorts out into the Pentland Firth for a full-calibre shoot with the 12-inch guns. According to Marine Albert Lee in *Inflexible*, the fall of shot around the target was 'spotted' by observers in balloons moored to two balloon ships. The results of firing, he reported, 'were highly satisfactory'. By 3.45 p.m. the Squadron was back at anchor inside the Flow, coaling and preparing for night firing with the 4-inch guns, which was scheduled to take place that night. They were due to return to Rosyth on the following morning. It wasn't to be.

At 5.16 p.m. Jellicoe and Beatty received an Admiralty signal informing them that intercepted German signals indicated that the Germans intended an operation which would commence on the following morning, and that the High Seas Fleet would be leaving the Jade via the eastern route through the minefields in the Bight and out past the Horn Reefs light ship. 'Operation appears to extend over

May 31st and June 1st,' the signal read. 'You should concentrate to the eastward of the Long Forties ready for eventualities.' [The Long Forties lie about sixty miles east of the Scottish coast.]

Hood received from Jellicoe in *Iron Duke* the flag signal to raise steam for 22 knots at 6.25 p.m. His instructions were for the 3rd Battle Cruiser Squadron, screened by the destroyers *Shark, Acasta, Ophelia* and *Christopher*; and in company with the light cruisers *Chester* and *Canterbury*, to take up station ten miles ahead of the Grand Fleet as an advanced scouting screen. If the sweep came to nothing Hood was to rejoin the battlecruiser fleet at 2.30 p.m. on the following afternoon, at a rendezvous Jellicoe had arranged with Beatty, 100 miles off the Jutland coast. 'Just another sweep I expect,' Albert Lee wrote in his diary. By 11.00 p.m. that night both the Grand Fleet and the battle cruiser fleet had cleared their bases and were heading east through the darkness for the rendezvous. In all there were 28 battleships, nine battlecruisers, eight armoured cruisers, 26 light cruisers, 78 destroyers, one minelayer and one seaplane carrier, which made up the 151 warships of the greatest fleet the world had ever seen.

By 2.00 p.m. on the afternoon of 31 May, *Invincible* was approaching the position where she was due to turn south with her squadron for the rendezvous with the battlecruiser fleet. She was now twenty-miles ahead of the fleet, which had fallen astern of station, having been delayed by the customary examination of merchant and fishing vessels encountered on the way. Shortly before *Invincible* was about to turn south, *Indomitable* signalled to Hood: 'Have just heard Telefunken signals, very loud.' Almost simultaneously, *Invincible* intercepted a message from the light cruiser *Galatea*, which was with the battlecruiser fleet, reporting the sighting of two enemy cruisers. This was followed within the next 35 minutes (2.33 p.m. – 3.08 p.m.) by six other signals from *Galatea*, reporting seven enemy ships steering north. All the indications were that Beatty had made contact with enemy light forces which would, owing to the danger of having their line of retreat towards the Horn Reefs cut off, now endeavour to escape by heading north for the Skagerrak. Hood, who was not far off the entrance to the Skagerrak, increased speed to 22 knots at 3.11 p.m. and steered ESE, with the intention of cutting off the enemy's retreat. It was anticipated that contact would be made at about 4.00 p.m. Accordingly, 'Action' was sounded off in *Invincible* at 3.18 p.m.

Twenty minutes later the situation was dramatically changed when *Invincible* received another signal, this time from Beatty's flagship, *Lion*, reporting five enemy battle-cruisers in sight, followed by another two signals to the effect that he was engaging the enemy on a south-easterly course. Without informing Jellicoe or waiting for instructions from him, Hood seized the initiative and swung his squadron round onto a south-south-easterly course at 4.06 p.m. and tore off to support Beatty at full speed. At this juncture, the battlecruiser fleet bore fifty miles south-west of *Invincible* and as Hood's three battlecruisers had no margin of speed, his only chance of catching up was by steering a converging course of south-south-east on Beatty's course of south-east. For the next three-quarters of an hour no further signals were received. At 4.56 p.m. with *Invincible* and her consorts foaming through an empty sea at 26 knots, without sight or sound of the battle which was raging somewhere to the southward, Hood sent a radio message to Beatty requesting his position, course and speed. There was no reply. What was happening?

When Beatty sighted the German battlecruisers at 3.30 p.m. he swung the 1st and 2nd Battle Cruiser Squadrons around onto a south-easterly course, with the object of getting between the enemy and his base. Vice-Admiral Franz von Hipper, in his flagship *Lützow*, conformed with Beatty's turn and for the next 51 minutes a running fight ensued on parallel courses. The five German battlecruisers were out-numbered two to one by Beatty's six battlecruisers and the four immensely powerful fast battleships of the 5th Battle Squadron [although the latter were out of range when fire was opened at 3.47 p.m. and did not come into action until eighteen minutes later at 4.06 p.m.]. Beatty had a crushing superiority, which surely spelt annihilation for the German battlecruisers.

Barham	32 × 15-inch guns	Lützow	16 × 12-inch guns
Valiant		Derfflinger	
Warspite		Seydlitz	28 × 11-inch guns
Malaya		Moltke	
Lion	32 × 13.5-	Von der Tann	
Princess Royal	inch guns		
Queen Mary			
Tiger			
New Zealand	12 × 12-inch		
Indefatigable	guns		

Total weight of broadside
= 111,640 pounds.

Total weight of broadside
= 33,104 pounds.

[These figures discount the guns that could not be brought to bear on the broadside.]

In view of this great material superiority it is all the more incredible that during this phase of the Battle of Jutland (3.47 p.m. to 4.36 p.m.) which has become known as the 'Run to the South', the weaker German force actually inflicted a partial defeat on Beatty.

Although the visibility was a mitigating factor (the light-grey German ships merged into the dull-grey sky behind them, while Beatty's ships were silhouetted against a clear horizon to the westward), the British were quite simply outgunned by superior German gunnery efficiency. From opening fire at 3.47 p.m. until cease fire at 4.36 p.m., when the action was temporarily broken off, the Germans scored 44 hits (42 on the battlecruisers and two on *Barham*), while in return they received only seventeen hits (eleven from the battlecruisers and six from the 5th B.S.). Even when the British gunners scored a hit they were robbed of their rewards because of defective armour-piercing shells. [The Ordnance Board's Professor of Statistics calculated that 30–70 per cent of the shells were duds.] In comparison, the German shells wrought havoc. At 4.02 p.m. two 11-inch shells fired by *Von der Tann* at *Indefatigable* at a range of 16,000 yards, tore through the thin side plating [above the armoured belt] abreast 'X' turret, *and in all probability* penetrated the 1-inch armour of the main deck and the 3-inch armour at the base of the barbette leading from the magazine to 'X' turret, where it exploded.

Indefatigable did not follow in the wake of *New Zealand*, which was turning to port, but began to go down by the stern. With phenomenal accuracy the gunners in *Von der Tann* hit *Indefatigable* again with two shells of the next salvo; one hit on the forecastle and the other on 'A' turret. The shells pierced the armour and exploded in the interior of the ship. Thirty seconds later the tremendous effect of these hits became apparent. Starting forward, flames and smoke gushed out of the hull and great fragments of the ship, including a 50-foot steam picket boat, intact though upside down, were hurled 200 feet into the air. Rolling over to port she sank, taking 57 officers and 960 men down with her. Twenty-four minutes later, at 4.26 p.m., *Queen Mary* was struck by two 12-inch shells from *Derfflinger* at a range of about 15,000 yards. One hit the fore-part of the ship and the other 'Q' turret. *In all probability* one shell tore through the thin deck plating of the forecastle and the 1-inch armour of the upper deck, exploding in or near the magazines of 'A' and 'B' turrets. The resulting explosion completely destroyed the fore-part of the ship as far aft as the main mast. Simultaneously, the shell that hit 'Q' turret penetrated the armour and caused an explosion of the cordite in the working chamber below the gun-house.

An observer stationed in the gun control position aloft on the foremast of *New Zealand* remembers 'passing the stern of a ship projecting about seventy feet out of the water, with the propellers revolving slowly . . . clouds of paper were blowing out of the after-hatch, and on her stern I read *Queen Mary*. We passed her about 100 yards on our port beam, and a moment later there was a blinding flash, a dull heavy roar, which ceased as suddenly as it began, followed by a few seconds' silence, and then the patter of debris.' All that was left of *Queen Mary* was a great mushroom-shaped cloud of smoke, 600 to 800 feet high. Fifty-seven officers and 1,209 men went down with her. Fisher's belief that 'speed is armour' had proved to be devastatingly foolish. 'The loss of the two Battle Cruisers', wrote Beatty in 1934, 'was not the fault of anybody in them, poor souls, but of faulty design . . . Their ships were too stoutly built whereas ours went up in a blue flame on the smallest provocation.' Not only was the scale of armour protection indifferent but, according to an officer who served on the Ordnance Board, 'The armour plate was also of an inferior quality.' In comparison, when the Run to the South came to an end at 4.36 p.m., the fighting efficiency of all five heavily armoured German battlecruisers was unimpaired. Four minutes after the destruction of *Queen Mary*, the light cruiser *Southampton*, scouting three miles ahead of *Lion*, sighted the German battle fleet steering northwards: sixteen battleships, six predreadnoughts, six light cruisers and 31 destroyers. At 4.46 p.m., Beatty turned the battlecruiser fleet north-west to lead the unsuspecting Germans onto the Grand Fleet, sixty miles to the north-west.

We left *Invincible* at 4.56 p.m., proceeding on a SSE course, trying to catch up with Beatty some fifty miles to the south. The dispositions of Hood's force were:

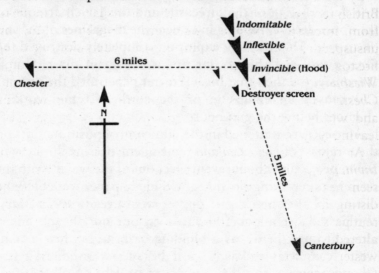

For the next thirty-four minutes Hood continued on his course, still without sight or sound of the battlecruiser fleet. All the while visibility was decreasing as *Invincible* nosed forward into thick patches of mist. 'On some bearings,' says Captain Kennedy of *Indomitable*, 'we could see 16,000 yards, while on other bearings visibility was down to 2,000 yards.' Then, suddenly, at 5.30 p.m., the sound of gun-fire was heard to the south-west along with gun flashes stabbing the mist [it was, in fact, the German battlecruisers, fourteen miles distant, engaging the 5th Battle Squadron on a north-westerly course]. The light cruiser, *Chester*, which was six miles off *Invincible*'s starboard beam, turned south-west and went off to investigate. Hood, still believing Beatty to be somewhere ahead of his south-south-east course, held on in that direction [*Lion* was, in fact, twenty miles west-south-west of *Invincible*]. Six minutes later (5.36 p.m.), *Chester* sighted the dim shapes of a three-funnelled cruiser and two destroyers steering north through the mist, 11,000 yards off her starboard bow. At first, it was assumed that this cruiser could be one of Beatty's scouts. It was, in fact, the German light cruiser *Frankfurt*, stationed five miles north-west on the disengaged side of the German battlecruisers.

By answering the challenge signalled by *Chester* with the British recognition signal [which the Germans had discovered from intercepted wireless messages], *Frankfurt* drew an unsuspecting *Chester* to within 6,000 yards before opening fire together with the rest of her Squadron, *Pillau, Elbing* and *Wiesbaden*, which suddenly broke out of the mist into *Chester*'s view. She was quickly smothered in a hail of shells and within five minutes three of her guns were disabled, leaving only one that could be brought to bear.

At 5.40 p.m. these flashes of gunfire were seen from *Invincible* in the direction from which *Chester* had last been seen heading into the mist. Although no ships could be distinguished from the flagship's bridge, or from Dannreuther's position high up in the fore-top, Hood immediately altered course hard to starboard and assumed a north-westerly course towards the gun flashes. A few minutes later *Chester* reappeared, 6,000 yards off *Invincible*'s port beam, surrounded by a forest of shell splashes. Moments later the phantom-like outlines of the four German cruisers appeared and at 5.53 p.m. *Invincible*'s 12-inch guns roared in anger for the first time since the Falklands battle. Two minutes later *Inflexible* and *Indomitable* opened five at a range of 12,000 yards. The cannonade lasted for only eight minutes before fire was checked at 6.00 p.m., when the four German cruisers put their helms over hard-a-starboard, fired torpedoes (without effect) and escaped southward into the mist and clouds of dense white smoke in which they enveloped themselves by igniting smoke boxes. As they turned, *Invincible* scored a hit on *Wiesbaden*, the rear ship of the German line. The shell exploded in *Wiesbaden*'s engine room, completely disabling her, by putting both her engines out of action. *Inflexible* also managed to score one hit on *Pillau*. Entering the stoke-holds through the foremost funnel, it ignited the coal and oil, which put four of her eight boilers out of action. She managed to maintain enough steam, however, to escape with the remainder of her squadron. Although *Wiesbaden* was now hidden by the smoke and mist from the sights of the gunners in the three battlecruisers, she was left helpless and began to drift out of control to westward and onto the guns of the Grand Fleet, which was approaching from the north-west. The one hit from *Invincible* sealed her fate. As the battle fleet passed, *Wiesbaden* was subjected to a cannonade in which more than 200 rounds were fired at her by guns of all calibres. She was left a burning wreck, but she did not finally succumb to the waves until about 2.00 a.m. the following morning.

In company with *Frankfurt*, *Pillau*, *Elbing* and *Wiesbaden* when they engaged *Chester*, were the 31 destroyers of the German 9th Flotilla, 2nd Flotilla and 12th Flotilla. Commencing at 5.55 p.m. these three flotillas launched attacks on *Invincible* and her squadron. Luckily the force of these attacks were blunted and confused by Hood's four screening destroyers, *Shark*, *Acasta*, *Ophelia* and *Christopher*, which although greatly outnumbered gallantly met the attacks head-on. First, the five destroyers of the 12th Half-Flotilla attacked at a range of 6,500 yards. They succeeded in firing only six torpedoes, one of which was aimed at one of the British destroyers. Next came the 9th Flotilla of ten destroyers, but the retiring 12th Half-Flotilla got in their way and, being also engaged by Hood's four destroyers, fired only three torpedoes at the battlecruisers. Only four destroyers of the 2nd Flotilla attacked and their effort consisted of one torpedo fired at a range of about 7,000 yards. In all, nine torpedoes were fired at the three battlecruisers. Simultaneous with the appearance of the German destroyers breaking out of the mist and smoke, Hood sighted Beatty's battlecruisers to westward, heavily engaged with an unseen enemy hidden in the mist to the south.

Turning his squadron due west to close Beatty, *Invincible* and her two consorts were broadside on when the torpedo attacks were launched. At 6.13 p.m. observing the tracks of the approaching torpedoes, Captain Cay turned *Invincible* hard to starboard away from the attack. As she turned, the helm jammed with the result that she had to stop, let her steam escape through the safety pipes and hoist the 'disregard' signal until she was brought under control. In the fore-top Dannreuther saw several torpedoes coming towards the ship, but to his relief they all passed harmlessly. As *Invincible* began her turn to starboard, *Inflexible* turned to port to comb the oncoming torpedoes. One, travelling very slowly, being near the end of its run, passed down the port side of the ship twenty feet away. Another passed astern, while a third, fortunately set too deep, passed right under her. Meanwhile, Captain Kennedy followed the flagship's example and met the attack by turning *Indomitable* to port. As she turned, two torpedoes, also travelling very slowly, passed close to her stern.

Having successfully countered the torpedo attack and gained control of her jammed helm, *Invincible* got under way again, course west, leading *Inflexible* and *Indomitable* in line ahead at twenty knots. At 6.20 p.m., two and a half hours since pressing forward to support Beatty, the situation at last became clear to Hood. Approaching *Invincible* head-on at 4,000 yards distance were Beatty's battlecruisers in action with the German battlecruisers, visible for the first time from

105

Invincible, 11,000 yards to the south-west. Behind Beatty the 28 battleships of the Grand Fleet were deploying into a 6-mile-long line of battle, surrounded by swarms of attendant destroyers and cruisers. At 6.22 p.m. Hood swung *Invincible* through 180° to starboard and took up station 3,000 yards ahead of *Lion* on a south-easterly course. And so it was that a ship designed to hunt down armed merchant cruisers and marauding cruisers much weaker than herself, now found herself as the leading ship of the battle fleet and about to become engaged with vastly superior battlecruisers and the powerful battleships heading the van of the German fleet. *Invincible* was steaming into annihilation.

Invincible now found herself on a parallel course with the five German battlecruisers, 9,000 yards off the starboard beam. During the run to the north Hipper's battlecruisers had suffered a further fifteen hits. *Lützow*, *Derfflinger* and *Seydlitz* were down by the bows, while *Von der Tann*'s guns were all temporarily disabled. Only *Moltke* was relatively unscathed. As Beatty's battlecruisers were engaging the rear three ships of Hipper's line, Hood's Squadron concentrated their fire on the two leading German battlecruisers, *Lützow* and *Derfflinger*. At 6.26 p.m. *Invincible* opened fire on *Lützow*. *Inflexible* also concentrated her fire on *Lützow*, while *Indomitable* ranged in on Derfflinger.

Twenty-one-year-old Marine gunner, Bryan Gasson, was at the rangefinder in *Invincible*'s 'Q' turret [under the command of Major Robert Colquhoun]. 'I was in a small compartment at the back of the turret,' Gasson recalls, 'my head sticking through a hole in the roof, working my rangefinder which was mounted on top of the turret.' *Lützow* was swathed in smoke and mist, but Gasson had a fairly clear view of her, magnified as she was twenty times in the stereoscopic sights of his rangefinder.

Within the next eight minutes *Invincible* scored eight hits on *Lützow* at a range of 9,600 yards. [It is estimated that she fired approximately fifty shells in this period.] A phenomenal piece of gunnery which inspired Admiral Hood on the bridge of *Invincible* to communicate with Dannreuther in the fore-top, congratulating him with the words: 'Your firing is very

good, keep at it as quickly as you can, every shot is telling.'
Dannreuther passed the message to the turrets. And 'tell' it
did. Two of *Invincible*'s eight hits found their mark on the
bow section of the 26,000-ton *Lützow* below the waterline.
Penetrating the hull below the armoured belt, they exploded
with devastating effect. Two thousand tons of seawater
poured in through the gaping holes, flooding the forward
sections and finding its way into the forward magazine
through an emergency exit which had been blown open by
the blast. With the sea washing over the fore-deck and
sinking by the bows, the stricken *Lützow* hauled out of line
and limped out of range of *Invincible*'s devastating fire into
the smoke and mist to the south. Although she had been hit a
total of twenty-four times by heavy shell in the course of the
battle, it was these two hits by *Invincible* which sank her.
Lützow struggled on until 2.00 a.m. the following morning.
A last attempt to steam stern first, so as to relieve the pressure
on the forward bulkheads, had to be abandoned when the
propellers came out of the water and the draught forward
increased to 56 feet. With 8,000 tons of water in the ship, she
was in imminent danger of capsizing, so Captain Harder gave
the order to abandon ship. Two torpedoes from the German
destroyer *G-38* delivered the *coup de grâce*.

During the eight-minute engagement, *Invincible* came
under the concentrated fire of both *Lützow* and *Derfflinger*.
Range taker, Able Seaman Ernest Dandridge, who was in the
fore-top with Dannreuther and Chief Petty Officer Walter
Thompson, recalls that: 'The first German salvoes fell about
1,200 yards short, but they gradually fell closer until they
were straddling the *Invincible*, deluging the ship with shell
splashes while pieces of shrapnel buzzed over the ship.' From
his position on the bridge of *Indomitable*, Captain Kennedy
saw a salvo hit *Invincible*'s after part but, apparently it
caused no appreciable damage. A minute later, at 6.34 p.m.,
a salvo from *Derfflinger* hit *Invincible* amidships. Bryan
Gasson, at the rangefinder in 'Q' turret, saw the salvo coming
and it is his distinct recollection that one shell hit the turret
between the guns. Penetrating the 7-inch face armour, it
exploded in the gun-house killing all the Marines except

Midship Section of *Invincible*, looking forward

The magazine fed both 'P' and 'Q' turrets.

Upper deck

Main deck

Lower deck

No. 8 cabin

Seamen's wash place

P.O.'s Wash place

Trunk for embarking 12 inch ammunition

Coal bunker 1½in

Fire wood

Coal bags

Gunners stores 1½in

Coal bunker

'P' Turret

Barbette

7in

7in

3in

7in

7in

6in

Coal bunker

2in

1½in

2½in

Coal bunker

Hoist from shell room and magazine to gun turret

Tunnel for steam pipes

Air space

Handling room

12 inch shell room

Air space

Tunnel for steam pipes

113,520 lbs of cordite at full load

12 inch magazine (cordite)

440 shells at full load

12 inch shell room

12 inch shell room

12 inch shell room

Watertight compartment

Coal bunker

2½in

2in

6in

1in

Gasson and blowing the turret roof off. From his position in the fore-top Dannreuther saw the roof of the turret blown off by the explosion and hurled over the side of the ship. There are two *possible* explanations as to what happened next. Either the explosion in the turret ignited the ammunition there, and the resultant flash and flame roared down the 60-foot hoist into the magazine; or another shell from the same salvo hit *Invincible* amidships, either on the side of the hull above the armour belt or on the deck, and plunged down through the thin deck armour and exploded directly in the magazine. There can be no certainty which it was, but the result would have been exactly the same. The midship magazine [feeding both 'P' and 'Q' turrets and separated from them by a thin bulkhead] lay transverse across practically the full beam of the ship. When either the flash from 'Q' turret or the shell entered this 'hostage to fortune' the resulting explosion was tremendous. The whole central section of the ship – including the boiler rooms, funnels, coal bunkers and the two midship turrets – was rent apart in a gigantic ball of crimson flame. Masses of coal-dust issued from the riven hull; the tripod masts collapsed, and the great ball of flame rose leisurely, contemptuously and with an awful majesty, 400 feet into the air. At its top was a picket boat, an immense baulk of ship's plating and many lesser bits. Then the deep red faded out and there remained only a black pall of smoke which slowly cleared to reveal *Invincible*'s bow and stern standing up out of the water. She had broken in half in thirty fathoms of water, and with the central section of the ship [from the foremast to the mainmast] completely destroyed, the inner parts of the two halves came to rest on the sea bed exposing fifty feet of the bow and stern: 'Stuck out of the sea like half-tide rocks, grim and awful in their separation.'

Invincible – Fisher's gem, his mighty greyhound of the sea, sank in an incredible thirty seconds, taking Rear-Admiral Hood, Captain Cay and 1,019 officers and men with her. Von Hase, *Derfflinger*'s Gunnery Officer, shouted into his telephone 'Our enemy has blown up!', and above the din of battle a great cheer thundered through the ship as Hase offered 'a short, fervent prayer of thanks to the Almighty'. Beatty, who had witnessed the destruction of *Invincible* from the bridge of *Lion* described his feelings to the 2nd Sea Lord three days later. 'You should have seen Hood bring up his Squadron into action, it would have done your heart good. No one could have died a more glorious death.' In the water between the two halves of the wreck, among a mass of kit-bags, hammocks, spars and other wreckage, were a mere six survivors. As *Inflexible* and *Indomitable* raced past, sheering over to port to avoid the wreck, they were cheered by some of the survivors. 'I have never seen anything more splendid', wrote an officer of *Indomitable*, 'than those few cheering us as we raced by them.'

'I didn't hear the explosion,' Bryan Gasson recollects. 'I can't remember it at all. It was too much for the mind to comprehend. The next thing I knew I was deep down in the water entangled in wreckage. Freeing myself I braced myself by standing to attention, so to speak, and surfaced in an air bubble. I saw the two ends sticking out of the water, and looked around for other people and to my surprise saw no one.'

Commander Dannreuther, Chief Petty Officer Thompson, and Able Seaman Dandridge, who had all been in the fore-top when the explosion occurred, were saved by the mast collapsing away from the ball of flame. 'The force of the explosion', Dandridge recalled, 'seemed to lift the centre of the ship right out of the sea, and it was only a matter of thirty seconds before I found myself struggling in the water. I had barely time to realize there had been an explosion before the ship was gone. I was thrown upon the rangefinder in one corner of the top. The rangefinder was smashed, and when the ship traversed I narrowly escaped being pinned to the side of the top by it, but I just managed to pull myself clear in time. I scrambled to the upper part of the top and dived out when the mast hit the water. When I came to the surface I was clear of the sinking ship, and almost choked with the water I had swallowed. Upon looking round I saw Chief Petty Officer Thompson. He called out to me and pointed to some floating wreckage. I grasped a kit-bag and clung to it for a while. Then a target which had floated from the *Invincible* came along and I climbed upon it, where Thompson joined me. Shortly afterwards, Commander Dannreuther and Lieutenant Sandford [who had escaped through the open hatch of the Fore Conning Tower when the ship went down] also scrambled on to the target. Another man who had succeeded in getting clear of the fore-top when the mast collapsed into the sea, struck out for the target but with floundering arms he drowned before he could reach us. Whilst we were in the water the battle still raged and shells kept falling in the sea around us. Several times we were drenched by the wash of big ships which went racing past and sending their stern waves rolling over the target. The water was fairly smooth, though very cold, and from being so frequently "washed down" we felt this very much.'

Supporting himself on a smaller target, some distance away from the four men, was another survivor: Yeoman of Signals Walter Pratt. He had been on the Director Tower platform on the foremast just below the fore-top. But they didn't see Bryan Gasson who was clinging to a mess stool. Having recovered from the initial shock of his miraculous escape, he now realized that he was badly burnt about his hands, arms and head; and that all his clothes had been burnt off. As it was not British practice for warships to stop and pick up survivors while in action, the chances of rescue for these six men were remote. Luckily, when Beatty passed by the wreck at 6.40 p.m. and saw the men in the water, he ordered the destroyer *Badger*, by signal lamp, to 'pick up men from wreck of ship on starboard hand'.

When *Badger* approached the wreck at 7.00 p.m., Bryan Gasson remembers seeing her slip a boat, and how, with his last ounce of strength [he had been in the water for twenty-five minutes and, being naked, was feeling extremely cold] waved his arms to attract their attention. To his relief the boat made for him. After being lifted into *Badger*'s boat, he became unconscious and remained so for four days. When he came to he found himself in the Hospital Ship *Plassy*. [He was transferred to the Edinburgh Royal Infirmary shortly afterwards and did not return to active service until twelve months later.) An officer of *Badger* relates how, 'Assuming this to be a German wreck and that we should have prisoners to pick up, I sent to have an armed guard detailed, and warned our doctor to be ready to tend wounded prisoners. A few minutes later I received exactly similar orders from the Captain. In the meantime, we had cut through a gap between the battlecruisers, and were heading towards the wreck in "no man's land" between the two fleets. As we neared the wreck we could see the water all round thick with flotsam and jetsam, mainly composed of seamen's kit-bags, with a few hammocks scattered amongst them. We also spotted a raft on which were four men, and on the bridge they spotted two other survivors in the water.

By orders from the Captain I lowered and sent away the whaler with our gunner in charge armed with a service revolver. The Captain brought the ship alongside the raft, and I waited with the doctor and the armed guard to receive German survivors. Judge of my surprise when the raft was almost alongside, to see a Commander R.N., a Lieutenant R.N. and two seamen ratings on it. In my surprise I forgot to dismiss the armed guard who, no doubt considering that it was that for which they were there, wanted to seize on the unfortunate survivors as we hauled them on board. However, I quickly sent the guard away and apologised to the Commander, who only treated it as a good joke. It was a great shock to us when he made us understand that the wreck we were near was the remains of the *Invincible*, and that we were picking up the only six survivors from her ship's company of a thousand men. The Commander (Dannreuther) was marvellously self-possessed. I can hardly understand to this day how a man, after going through what he had, could come on board from the raft as cheerily as if he was simply joining a new ship. He had merely – as he put it – stepped into the water when the foretop came down.' According to Dandridge, *Badger* then lowered a second boat to pick up Pratt, whom Dannreuther pointed out drifting some distance off.

While *Badger* was picking up the survivors, Jellicoe passed by in his flagship *Iron Duke*. By signal lamp the flagship inquired 'Is wreck one of our own ships.' To which *Badger* made the sad reply, 'Yes. *Invincible*.' While *Iron Duke* was passing by on the port side of the wreck, Vice-Admiral Doveton Sturdee passed by on the starboard side in the battleship *Benbow*. What Sturdee's feelings were on seeing the sad remains of his old Falklands flagship are unrecorded. The last ship of the fleet to pass the wreck was the light cruiser *Galatea*, at 7.30 p.m. She observed the stern section of *Invincible* sink, leaving the bow section still fifty feet out of the water. By 5.00 a.m. on the dull, overcast morning of 1 June, the German Fleet, having evaded action with the Grand Fleet in the mist shortly after the loss of *Invincible*, entered the swept channel south-west of Horn Reefs, steering for the Jade. With all hope of bringing the Germans to battle gone, Jellicoe turned the fleet north-west at 10.00 a.m. and headed back to Scapa. Beatty and the battlecruiser fleet swept north in search of any disabled enemy ships. At 2.35 p.m. *Galatea*, which had observed *Invincible*'s stern section sink on the previous evening, discovered the bow still standing out of the water. The sea had given up some of *Invincible*'s dead, for several bodies were seen floating around the wreck. After the battlecruiser fleet had passed, Lieutenant-Commander Curt Beitzen, Captain of the German submarine *U-75*, sighted the bow section through his periscope. He was the last man to observe the wreck of *Invincible* above water.

On arriving at Scapa on the afternoon of Friday, 2 June, Jellicoe ordered the submarine tender *Titania*, stationed at Blyth, to 'send a submarine as soon as weather permits [a heavy gale had been blowing from the north-west since the evening of 1 June] to sink by torpedo, gunfire or explosive charge, the portion of the wreck of *Invincible* in approximately latitude 57° 06' North, Longitude 6° 02' East, if still showing above water, in order to guard against the risk of secret documents being recovered by the enemy.' Accordingly, the submarine *G-10* sailed from Blyth at 3.00 a.m. on the morning of Saturday, 3 June, and searched the area for forty-eight hours. Nothing was found, and it was considered that the bow section had sunk during the gale. The steel headstone that had marked the watery grave of 1,021 sailors had disappeared forever.

Three years later, Captain J. E. T. Harper was commissioned by the Admiralty to compile an official record of the Battle of Jutland. During his investigations, Harper came to the conclusion that both *Iron Duke* and *Lion* were out in their dead reckoning. This made it difficult to chart the course of the battle with any degree of accuracy. On 17 April 1919, therefore, Harper submitted a memorandum to The Deputy Chief of the Naval Staff to the effect that: 'If possible, the wreck of *Invincible* be located and the position be fixed, the geographical position of the British Battle Fleet at Jutland will be ascertained beyond doubt, as the 3rd and 4th Divisions of the Battle Fleet passed one on either side of the wreck at about 6.57 p.m. The position of the wreck as given by the C in C, in his report, is Lat 57° 04' N, Long 6° 02' E, but after having weighed all the evidence available in the logs and reports of the ships present at Jutland, it is considered that Lat 57° 3¼' N, Long 6° 07¾' E is more likely to be the correct position. The Latitude being, in all probability, more correct than the Longitude.' On 3 July 1919, the wreck was indeed located by a minesweeper, sent out under the command of Commander Bell, who fixed the position as Latitude 57° 02' 40" North, Longitude 6° 07' 15" East, almost exactly where Harper believed it would be found. And there she remains undisturbed, a silent war grave on the Jutland bank, thirty fathoms under the restless waves of the North Sea.

Appendices

DIMENSIONS

Length	530ft ¾in pp, 562ft 6in wl, 567ft oa
Beam	78ft 6in
Draught	24ft 7in (forward), 27ft (aft), 29ft 7in (deep load)

DISPLACEMENT

Legend	17,250 tons
Actual	17,330 tons
Deep load	19,940 tons
Sinkage	69.8 tons per inch
Weight of hull	6,022 tons

FREEBOARD

Forward	30ft
Amidships	22ft
Aft	17ft 2in

PROTECTION

Main belt	6in (from a little forward of 'A' turret to the centreline of 'X' turret)
Width of belt	4ft 1in below water, 7ft 3in above waterline
Barbettes	7in (2in below level of belt)
Turrets	7in (face, sides and rear)
	3in (roofs and rear floor)
Conning tower forward	10in (2in roof)
Conning tower aft	6in (2in roof)
Magazine screens	2½in
Main deck	¾in forward
	1in beneath forward and midships barbettes

Lower deck forward 1½in on flats and slopes
Lower deck amidships 1½in on flats
                    2in on slopes
Lower deck aft   2½in on flats and slopes

MACHINERY
Four Parsons Turbines (SHP 41,000) = 25.5 knots. (On the measured mile *Invincible* achieved 46,500 SHP = 26.64 knots)
Thirty-one large-tube Yarrow boilers
Cost of machinery £472,000

FUEL

Coal	1,000 tons (normal load)
	3,084 tons (maximum load)
Oil	738 tons
Radius of action	2,270 nautical miles at 23 knots
Coal consumption	790 tons per day at 25 knots
	130 tons per day at 10 knots

FRESH WATER
350 tons

COMPLEMENT

1908	730
1914	799
1916	1,032

SEARCHLIGHTS
Eight 36in
One 24in

ANCHORS

Bower	3 (Wasteney Smith stockless, 125cwt)
Stream	1 (Martin's close-stowing, 42cwt)
Kedge	1 (as stream)
Admiralty Pattern	2 (5cwt)

BOATS

2 × 50ft Steam Pinnace	1 × 40ft Steam Barge
1 × 42ft Launch	1 × 36ft Sailing Pinnace
3 × 32ft Cutters	1 × 32ft Galley

1 × 30ft Gig	3 × 27ft Whalers
2 × 16ft Dinghies	1 × 13ft Raft

MAIN ARMAMENT
Eight 12in, 45 cal, BL, Mk X

Gun axis 12in guns	'A' turret 32ft
	'P' and 'Q' turrets 28ft
	'X' turret 21ft
Weight of gun	56 tons 16 cwt
Weight of one mounting	335 tons (excluding guns)
Length of gun	57ft
Muzzle velocity	2,725 feet per second
Maximum rate of fire	two shells per minute
Maximum range	16,500 yards (increased to 19,000 yards when 4CRH shells were supplied in 1915–16. CRH = Calibre Radius Head. These shells were more sharply pointed and, encountering less air resistance, were able to travel farther.)
Weight of shell	850lb
Weight of cordite charge	258lb
Rounds per gun	Peace time outfit: 80 (24 Armour-Piercing, 40 Common Pointed (both black powder filled) and 16 High-Explosive shells filled with Lyddite. Wartime outfit: 110 (33 Armour-Piercing shells (Lyddite filled), 38 Common Pointed and 39 High-Explosive.
Practice shells	24

SECONDARY, ANTI-DESTROYER GUNS
Sixteen 4in Mk III quick-firing

Weight of gun	1 ton 6 cwt
Length of gun	13ft 9¼in
Muzzle velocity	2,300 feet per second
Maximum rate of fire	20 shells per minute
Weight of shell	25lb
Weight of charge	3lb 9oz
Maximum range	9,000 yards

Rounds per gun   100 (1,824 total rounds carried: Steel
                    Common 800, Lyddite Common 800,
                    Practice 224)

TORPEDOES
Five 18in submerged tubes (four broadside and one stern)
Torpedoes   23

APPENDIX 2. COMPARISON OF THE MAIN FEATURES OF *INVINCIBLE* AND *DERFFLINGER*

	INVINCIBLE	DERFFLINGER
Displacement	17,330 tons	26,180 tons
Length	567ft (oa)	690ft 3in (oa)
Beam	78ft 6in	95ft 1¾in
Speed	41,000 SHP = 25 knots	76,600 SHP = 28 knots
Armament	Eight 12in	Eight 12in
Weight of shell	850lb	893lb
Maximum range	16,500 yards	22,300 yards
Armour:		
Main belt	6in	12in
Upper belt	Nil	8in
Belt at bow	4in	5in
Belt at stern	Nil	5in
Magazine screens	2½in	6in
Turret front plates	7in	11in
Turret roofs	3in	3.2in
Protective decks	¾in–2½in	1in–3¼in
Weight of armour	3,460 tons	9,890 tons

APPENDIX 3. SUMMARY OF *INVINCIBLE*'S CAREER 1909–14

20 March 1909	Ship secured to South Railway Jetty. Commissioned by Captain M. E. F. Kerr, for service in the 1st Cruiser Squadron, Home Fleet.
1 April 1909	Proceeded to the Firth of Forth, in company with *Dreadnought*.

7–21 April 1909	Manoeuvres with battle fleet in the North Sea.
5–14 May 1909	Gunnery trials in the Firth of Forth.
12 June 1909	Spithead Review: visit of the Imperial Press Conference.
15-17 June 1909	Manoeuvres with battle fleet in Western Approaches.
20 July 1909	Fleet review off Southend: Visit of the Lords Commissioners of the Admiralty and the Mayor of London.
31 July–9 August 1909	Spithead Review: King Edward VII and the Russian Royal Family. Anniversary of the Coronation of the King.
13 August–28 December 1909	Portsmouth dockyard, to have approved modifications made in the electrical fittings of the 12-inch turrets.
22 February 1910	Gunnery trials off Bantry Bay.
18–21 April 1910	Manoeuvres with 1st Cruiser Squadron, North Sea.
25–27 April 1910	Manoeuvres with battle fleet.
13–15 June 1910	Sub-calibre gunnery trials in Weymouth Bay.
23–27 June 1910	Refit and repairs Portsmouth dockyard.
9–18 July 1910	Manoeuvres with battle fleet in Western Approaches.
23 July 1910	PZ exercises off Mounts Bay.
29 July 1910	Fleet Review, Torbay, visit by King Edward VII.
29 October 1910	Gunnery trials, Killary Bay, firing Lyddite shell at Bills Rock.
28 November–1 December 1910	Manoeuvres with battle fleet.
19 January–4 February 1911	Manoeuvres with battle fleet, Spanish waters, off Arosa Bay and Vigo Bay.
27 March–22 May 1911	Alterations to the electrical fittings of the 12-inch turrets, and refit. Canvas blast screens fitted to rear of 4-inch guns in 'A' and 'X' turrets. Additional yard on fore-topmast.
28 March 1911	Captain R. P. E. Purefoy relieved Captain Kerr.
9 June 1911	Gunnery trials, English Channel.
15 June 1911	Spithead Review: Coronation review of King George V.

28 July– 24 August 1911	Manoeuvres with battle fleet in North Sea.
31 August– 1 September 1911	Heavy gun-layers test in the Moray Firth.
8 September– 10 October 1911	Exercises with 1st Cruiser Squadron in North Sea.
8–20 February 1912	Manoeuvres with battle fleet in Spanish waters, off Arosa Bay and Vigo Bay.
16–30 April 1912	Refit Portsmouth dockyard. 24-inch searchlight on platform under fore-top repositioned on roof of Admiral's Shelter, abaft fore-funnel. Two 36-inch searchlights added abreast fore-funnel at level of boat deck.
1 May 1912	Captain M. Culme-Seymour relieved Captain Purefoy.
4 May–24 July 1912	Exercises with 1st Cruiser Squadron on various dates, North Sea and Western Approaches.
7–24 September 1912	Visit with 1st Cruiser Squadron (*Lion, Inflexible, Indomitable* and *Indefatigable*) to Norway and Denmark. Trondheim (7th–10th), Molde (11th–12th), Oslo (13th–17th), Copenhagen (18th–24th). Ships visited by the Norwegian and Danish Royal Families.
7–10 October 1912	Gunnery practice off Cromarty.
21–23 October 1912	Manoeuvres off Torbay, with 1st, 2nd and 3rd Cruiser Squadrons.
5–28 November 1912	Refit Portsmouth dockyard.
12–19 February 1913	Manoeuvres with battle fleet, off Berehaven and Galway Bay.
17 March 1913	At anchor in Stokes Bay, Spithead. Submarine *C-34* collided with *Invincible*. No damage.
29 March 1913	Joined up with the newly constituted Battle Cruiser Squadron, at Berehaven.
3–7 April 1913	Sub-calibre firing off Berehaven.
8–17 April 1913	Manoeuvres with Battle Cruiser Squadron in Western Approaches.
29 April–2 May 1913	Gunnery trials in the Cromarty Firth with *Indomitable* and *Indefatigable*.

12, 15, 20, 22 May and 2 June 1913	Gunnery practice in North Sea.
23–31 July 1913	Manoeuvres with Battle Cruiser Squadron.
3 August 1913	Captain H. B. Pelly relieved Captain Culme-Seymour.
1 September–7 December 1913	With 2nd Battle Cruiser Squadron in the Mediterranean. Gibraltar (1–4 September). Cartagena (5–10 September). Valencia (11–15 September). Alcudia Bay, Majorca (16–22 September). Palma, Majorca (23–27 September). Gibraltar (29–8 October). Cartagena (9–11 October – Ship visited by the King of Spain and President Poincaré). Gibraltar (12–18 October). Palma Bay (20–25 October). Cagliari, Sardinia (26–29 October). Malta (30–8 November). Alexandria)21–26 November). Salamis Bay (28 November–3 December – Visit by the King of Greece). Malta (5–7 December). Arrived Portsmouth 13 December.
31 December 1913	Ship paid off, Portsmouth dockyard. 12-inch turrets converted to hydraulic motivation. 4-inch guns on roofs of 'A' and 'X' turrets removed and repositioned in casemates in forward superstructure. Two 4-inch guns fitted to shelter deck between fore-funnels. Two 4-inch guns fitted on platform abreast forward conning tower. All 4-inch guns in forward superstructure enclosed in casemates and fitted with shields. Rangefinder hood fitted to roof of 'A' turret. Gun director fitted on platform under foretop. New foretop, with 9-foot Argo rangefinder fitted. Searchlight platforms at level of navigating bridge extended and two 36-inch searchlights added. Bridge remodelled. Topmasts shortened and spiral rangefinder baffle fitted to fore-topmast.
4 August 1914	War declared.
16 August 1914	*Invincible* puts to sea from Portsmouth.

APPENDIX 4. PERSONAL MEMOIR OF MY SERVICE IN HMS *INVINCIBLE* BY CAPTAIN R. ROSS STEWART, RN.

My association with battlecruiser *Invincible* really began some six months before I actually joined her on the outbreak of war. I was serving in HMS *Monmouth*, a cruiser of the China Squadron. My previous sea service was in HMS *Good Hope*, a cruiser in the Channel Squadron, commanded by Admiral Sturdee. Well before the war started, HMS *Monmouth* was anchored in the Yangtze River, off the approaches to Shanghai, with the object of safeguarding British interests during fighting between North and South China. Among ships of other nations anchored there, were the German cruisers *Scharnhorst* and *Gneisenau*. We midshipmen struck up a friendship with our opposite numbers in the gunrooms of the two German ships, with whom we exchanged visits. Subsequently, after HMS *Monmouth* returned to her base in Hong Kong, I and other members of the gunroom were sent back to England to complete our courses for the rank of Sub-Lieutenant.

On the outbreak of war, I was appointed to HMS *Invincible* which was undergoing an extensive refit at Portsmouth. At first, I was much involved in preparing the ship for war. She had been hurriedly commissioned. A large number of the ship's company were reservists and a number of officers were drawn from shore establishments and the training service. When we put to sea we took with us a number of technicians from Vickers, who had yet to complete the installation of a new gunnery fore control and a new hydraulic system for gun turret working. They were all dedicated to bringing the ship to a state of readiness for action. As I write this short memoir of my service in *Invincible*, I recognize that my life in the Navy was enriched by my association with those officers and men who in such a short commission converted the ship to a magnificent unit, and gave up their lives when their task was completed.

In due course, *Invincible* joined the battlecruiser *New Zealand* in the River Humber and we did not have long to wait to test our guns. We first saw action in the Heligoland Bight, and I remember that it was through the mist in the early morning of 28 August 1914, that I saw the flash of enemy guns firing at us. Later in the year, news of the naval action off the Coronel coast of South America reached us. My two former ships, *Good Hope* and *Monmouth* had been sunk with all hands by those very ships, *Scharnhorst* and *Gneisenau*, with whom we had been fraternizing

122

such a short time before. With speed and secrecy a task force was formed under the command of Admiral Sturdee, consisting of *Invincible* as flagship, with her sister ship *Inflexible*, with orders to seek out and destroy the German squadron. On 8 December 1914, we arrived at Port Stanley in the Falkland Islands and immediately started coaling ship, a procedure in which *Invincible* had achieved a high state of efficiency, and in which all officers and men who did not have other duties took part. On this occasion, being a watchkeeper, and having the middle watch, I turned in at 4.00 a.m. while coaling was proceeding. At 8.00 a.m. my Marine servant called me with a cup of tea and the words 'You had better hurry up and get dressed, Sir, the Germans are outside and we are casting off the colliers. Sure enough, before disappearing into 'A' turret, my action-station, as *Invincible* gathered speed in chase, there on the horizon I could see the smoke of the German squadron desperately trying to escape. The story has been told many times of the action off the Falklands, but what has not been recorded is the twist of fate occasioned by grasping a hand in friendship on the China Sea and grasping the same hand in succour from the Atlantic Ocean such a short time later.

When we arrived back at our base in the Firth of Forth, the battlecruiser force was in the process of reorganization. There were to be three squadrons. Admiral Sir David Beatty took command of the whole force, and Admiral Sir Horace Hood hoisted his flag in *Invincible* to command the 3rd Battle Cruiser Squadron. Some time after, Admiral Hood assumed his command, and when a vacancy occurred, I became his Flag-Lieutenant, and a new phase of my duties began. My action-station was on the bridge with the Admiral. I remember slinging a hammock in the bridge structure outside Hood's sea cabin so as to be immediately available at any time during the night. Thus I was privileged to take part in the strategical and tactical preparations for the conduct of the Grand Fleet in their meeting with the German High Seas Fleet, which we all felt was imminent. They met at Jutland, when I was on leave from *Invincible*, and my ship, my Admiral, and my comrades were lost.

R. Ross Stewart,
Soberton, Hampshire.
January, 1986

APPENDIX 5. OFFICERS AND MEN MENTIONED IN CAPTAIN BEAMISH'S DISPATCH FOR SERVICES PERFORMED DURING THE ACTION OF THE FALKLAND ISLANDS, 8 DECEMBER 1914.

(Adm 137/304 folios 143–145)

'I would beg to bring to your notice the services of the following officers and men:

COMMANDER RICHARD HERBERT DENNY TOWNSEND,* who was constantly about the ship attending fires, etc., and although suffering much pain and hardly able to walk from a badly bruised foot caused by a bag rack falling on him when a shell burst near, he remained on duty to the last, and by his zeal and energy imbued everyone with a good spirit.

LIEUTENANT-COMMANDER HUBERT EDWARD DANNREUTHER, conducted the control of fire in a most able manner, exhibiting coolness and skill under an accurate and disturbing fire from the enemy. The fact that the recently converted turrets came so well through the ordeal speaks much for his untiring efforts to keep them well tuned up.

LIEUTENANT LANCELOT J. G. LEVESON, R.N.R., was of great service in dealing with the occasional troubles that occurred in the turrets, and by his great knowledge and skill helped materially towards the successful issue.

ENGINEER COMMANDER EDWARD JOHN WEEKS, who enabled every call on the propelling machinery to be instantly met, and by his skill in keeping everything efficient over several months of steaming enabled the revolutions to reach an average of 298 during one hour of the chase, and at one period worked up to 308 revolutions or 27 knots.

ENGINEER LIEUTENANT-COMMANDER JAMES FRASER SHAW, on seeing that dense smoke was coming into the Port Engine Room, went up and took charge of the Fire Brigade and by his skilful organization and promptitude put out a number of fires, and prevented many others occurring.

FLEET SURGEON WALTER JAMES BEARBLOCK,* who quickly met the emergency of dealing with the survivors from the *Gneisenau*, and undoubtedly saved many of their lives by his skill and organization.

MR THOMAS ANDREW WALLS,* CARPENTER, who exhibited skill and resource in dealing with the serious injury below the waterline, and thereby made the ship seaworthy.

ENGINE ROOM ARTIFICER 1ST CLASS GEORGE HENRY FRANCIS McCARTEN,* who, in order to save time and bring a gun into action in 'Q' turret with the least possible delay, entered the trunk under a jammed shell cage without waiting to hang the cage or support it, the cage wire being slack; he ran grave risk of personal injury and by his efforts cleared the jam and rendered the gun efficient with great celerity.

I would also beg to bring to your notice the case of LEADING SEAMAN FREDERICK MARTIN – Gunner's mate, Gunlayer 1st Class – who is stationed in 'X' turret. This turret is in charge of Lieutenant-Commander John C. F. Borrett,* and is uniformly efficient; it was especially so during the action of December the 8th. Martin is 25 years of age and has only not been made Petty Officer, for there is no vacancy, and I would therefore respectfully submit that I may have the authority to specially rate him Petty Officer as a reward for meritorious service. The efficiency of 'X' turret is largely due to the education, keeness and zeal of this man.

(P. T. H. Beamish, Captain HMS *Invincible*, 19 December 1914.)

*Those names marked with an asterisk were lost with the ship at Jutland.

APPENDIX 6. OFFICERS AND MEN LOST IN HMS *INVINCIBLE*, 6.34 p.m. 31 MAY 1916.

The ship's complement was 1,036; of these six survived the explosion, five men had deserted before the ship sailed to Scapa from Rosyth, and three men and one officer (Lieutenant R. R. Stewart) were on leave. Thus 1,021 were with the ship.

OFFICERS
(Those marked with an asterisk had served on the ship since her commissioning on 3 August 1914.)

Rear-Admiral, The Honourable Horace Lambert Alexander Hood, C.B., M.V.O., D.S.O.
Secretary Harold R. Gore Browne.
Lieutenant Frank P. O'Reilly.
Assistant Paymaster Lewis R. Tippen.
Clerk John M. Powell.

Captain Arthur Lindsay Cay.
Commander Richard Herbert Denny Townsend.*
Commander (N) Lionel H. Shore.*
Lieutenant-Commander John C. F. Borrett ('X' turret).*
Lieutenant-Commander Edward Smyth-Osborne ('P' turret).*
Lieutenant Alexander P. McMullen.
Lieutenant Thomas F. S. Flemming.
Lieutenant Alexander G. Murray.
Lieutenant George R. Hall, R.N.R.
Lieutenant Charles D. Fisher, R.N.V.R.
Engineer Commander Reuben Main.
Engineer Lieutenant Francis L. Mogg.*
Temporary Engineer Lieutenant John Hine.
Major Robert C. Colquhoun, R.M.L.I. ('Q' turret).*
Lieutenant John T. Le Seelleur, R.M.L.I.*
Chaplain the Revd. W. F. Morgan, B.A.
Naval Instructor John W. A. Steggall.
Fleet Paymaster Ernest W. L. Mainprice.*
Fleet Surgeon Walter J. Bearblock.
Surgeon Cyril O. H. Jones.
Surgeon George Shorland.
Sub-Lieutenant Alan G. Campbell-Cooke.
Acting Sub-Lieutenants Alexander Scrimgeour; Thomas H. Cobb; Leopold E. Johnstone; Alexander J. S. Richardson; Raymond S. Portal; William S. Hutchinson.
Engineer Sub-Lieutenant W. Hubert Unsworth.
Mate William T. Cory.
Mate (E) Samuel R. V. Self.
Assistant Paymaster Raymond A. Liversidge, R.N.R.
Chief Gunner William C. Hunt.*
Chief Bosun Frederick Luker.*
Acting Gunner Alfred J. Colton.
Gunner Mark W. Cameron.*
Gunner Ernest J. Read.*
Gunner William R. Roberts.

126

Acting Bosun William T. Donovan.
Signal Bosun William F. Raper.*
Royal Marine Gunner Albert E. Nixon.*
Warrant Telegraphist Ernest Kemp.
Carpenter Thomas A. Walls, D.S.O.*
Artificer Engineer Frederick C. Fry.*
Acting Artificer Engineer James Finlay.
Warrant Electrician Arthur C. Worthington.
Midshipmen Edward T. Hodgson.* John M. Shorland.* Richard
Henderson. Robin G. B. Giffard Brine. Cuthbert A. Hill. Douglas
A. C. Birch.* John H. G. Esmonde.* Desmond F. C. L. Tottenham.
Charles A. J. Acland-Hood.

MEN

Acting Gunner	1	Ship's Mate	1
Master-at-Arms	1	Ship's Corporals	4
Chief Petty Officers	4	Petty Officers	25
Leading Seamen	19	Able Seamen	151
Seamen	24	Ordinary Seamen	31
Boys	56	Sailmaker	1
Chief Yeomen of Signals	2	Yeomen of Signals	2
Leading Signalmen	5	Signalmen	13
Signal boys	6		
Petty Officer Telegraphist	2	Leading Telegraphist	1
Telegraphists	4	Boy Telegraphists	5
Chief Petty Officer Stokers	8	Petty Officer Stokers	30
Leading Stokers	57	Stokers	262
Chief Engineroom Artificers	9	Engineroom Artificers	23
Mechanicians	7		
Chief Electrical Artificers	2	Electrical Artificers	10
Wiremen	11		
Chief Shipwright	1	Shipwrights	7
Cooper	1	Plumbers	3
Painters	2	Blacksmiths	3
Chief Armourers	2	Armourers	4
Leading Carpenters	2	Carpenter's Crew	3

Joiner	1	Writers	3
Chief Ship's Cooks	2	Ship's Cooks	7
Officers' Chief Cook	1	Officers' Cooks	5
Officers' Chief Steward	1	Officers Stewards	13
Ship's Stewards	4	Chief Sick Berth Steward	1
Sick Berth Stewards	3	Sick Berth Attendant	1

MARINES

Sergeants	3	Corporals	4
Bombadiers	2	Gunners	22
Privates	59	Buglers	2
Bandmaster	1	Band Corporals	2
Musicians	14		

CIVILIANS

Canteen Managers	2	Canteen Assistants	2
Canteen Steward	1		

Officers	60
Men	961
Grand Total	1,021

The following officers and men were on leave:
Lieutenant R. R. Stewart. Able Seaman Elias Davies. Officers'
Steward Archie Hunter. Telegraphist Harold Carter.

Five men had deserted:
Able Seaman James McCauley. Able Seaman H. V. Jones. Ordinary
Seaman Michael Evans. Able Seaman Harold Charrington. Marine
Private Cecil Henry Wood.

The first four had given themselves up and were aboard the depot
ship *Crescent*, while Evans was arrested as a deserter by the police
the day before the ship was lost. His mother attempted to assist
Evans by making use of the fact that she had received a telegram
from the Admiralty wrongly listing him as being among those who
lost their lives.

There follows an example of the Admiralty acquaint sent to the
next of kin of the missing:

128

'Mrs. W. Pym,   Admiralty,
Penywain Street,   6th June 1916
Wainfelin,
Pontypool,
Monmouthshire,

Madam,
   I regret to have to inform you that HMS *Invincible* was sunk on
the 31st May, and that the name of your husband,
Rating: Able Seaman George Pym R.N.V.R. Official No. Wales
Z/789, Who is believed to have been on board, does not appear in
the lists of survivors received in this department. In these
circumstances it is feared that, in the absence of any evidence to the
contrary, he must be regarded as having lost his life.
Any application which the next of kin or legal representative may
have to make in consequence of the foregoing information should
be made by letter addressed to the Accountant General of the Navy,
Admiralty, London, S.W.'

   Twenty-four-year-old George Pym had joined the Royal Naval
Volunteer Reserve on 19 April 1915 as an Ordinary Seaman. He
was promoted to Able Seaman on 16 July 1915, and joined
Invincible at Rosyth on 20 August 1915.
   Shortly after the battle, the wife of Lieutenant-Commander
Borret wrote the following letter to Rear-Admiral Hood's widow.
Her daughter by her first marriage, Eleana Nickerson, in turn
passed it on to the mother of Alexander Scrimgeour.
   'I saw Commander Dannreuther, who was saved. You will love
to hear all that he has to tell us. I am writing fully because I gather
that you have not seen him yet, and don't want you to lose a minute
of the comfort that I got from his story. They were so pleased that
the moment had really come. In the *Invincible* they did not know
that the *Queen Mary* and *Indefatigable* had gone down. He
distinctly told me that he only heard it after he was saved. So they
had nothing to damp them. I think they first became engaged with a
light cruiser, then a pause, and they took on the *Derfflinger*. Your
husband (Hood) telephoned up to Commander Dannreuther: "The
firing is excellent. Keep it up as fast as you can; every shell is
telling." He passed the message on to the gun-turrets, and so my
darling in turret 'X' knew that they were giving satisfaction with
their guns. Then the crash came, and Commander Dannreuther
thinks the shock of the explosion killed them. Anyhow, there was

no struggle, no minute to think, because the ship sank in ten to fifteen seconds. He was in some high-up position with Leo (Acting Sub-Lieutenant Leopold Johnstone), and was thrown into the water some way off. He went down thirty feet and came up again at once, and when he reached the surface there was no one to be seen except the other five who were saved. I am so thankful that they had no minute to grieve or think of us. They were translated. I am writing all this fully because I want you to have with me the comfort of knowing that they were all so happy and satisfied up to the moment when they passed without feeling the passage into the next world. There is no separation in spirit, and I know we shall feel that more and more as the almost physical shock wears off us.'

APPENDIX 7. LIST OF BATTLE HONOURS AND H.M. SHIPS WHICH HAVE BORNE THE NAME *INVINCIBLE*

'*Invincible*' – 'Not to be conquered or subdued'.

1st Invincible
3rd rate ship-of-the-line. 74 guns. Crew 700. Displacement 1,793 tons. Length 171ft. Beam 49ft. Draught 21ft.
The French ship *L'Invincible*, captured as a prize in the battle off Cape Finisterre on 3 May 1747, and commissioned into the service of the Royal Navy as *Invincible*.
Wrecked during a gale on 19 February 1758, and sank on the Horse Tail Bank. No lives lost.

2nd Invincible
3rd rate ship-of-the-line. Built at Deptford. Launched 1765. 74 guns. Crew 600. Displacement 1,631 tons. Length 168ft. Beam 47ft. Draught 17ft.
1780. St. Vincent.
1782. St. Kitts.
1794. The Glorious First of June.
Wrecked during a gale on 16 March 1801, and sank on Hammonds Knowl off the Norfolk Coast. Captain Rennie and 400 men were drowned.

3rd Invincible
3rd rate ship-of-the-line. Launched at Woolwich in 1808. 74 guns. Crew 590. Displacement 1,674 tons. Length 170ft. Beam 48ft. Draught 18ft.

Broken up in 1861 after serving for some years, first as a powder vessel and then as a coal hulk at Devonport.

4th *Invincible*
Twin-screw, 14-gun broadside, Ironclad. Launched at Glasgow in 1869. Displacement 6,010 tons. 4,830hp. 14 knots. Length 280ft. Beam 54ft. Draught 23ft.
1882 Alexandria.
Name changed to *Fisgard* in 1904 and became a training establishment for boy artificers in Portsmouth harbour.
Foundered in a gale while under tow off Portland on 16 September 1914. 21 men were drowned.

5th *Invincible*
Battlecruiser *Invincible*.
1914 Heligoland Bight.
1914 Falkland Islands.
1916 Jutland.
31 May 1916, blew up at Jutland. 1,021 officers and men lost.

6th *Invincible*
Built at Barrow-in-Furness by Vickers. Cost £184.5 million.
Laid down 20 July 1973. Launched 3 May 1977.
Commissioned 11 July 1980.
Displacement 16,000 tons.
Length oa 677ft. Beam oa 105ft.
Draught 24ft.
Engines: 4 Olympus TM38 gas turbines. 2 shafts. Speed 28 knots.
Missiles: SAM: Twin Sea Dart.
Guns: Two Phalanx, two 20mm singles.
Aircraft: 5 Sea Harriers. 9 Sea King Helicopters (peace-time).
Complement: 1,100 (137 officers; 265 senior ratings; 604 junior ratings)
1982. Falkland Islands.

List of Sources

UNPUBLISHED ARCHIVE MATERIAL

PRO   Public Record Office
Adm   Admiralty Records
Cab   Cabinet Office Papers
NMM National Maritime Museum
IWM   Imperial War Museum
NL   Naval Library, Ministry of Defence
CCC   Churchill College, Cambridge

Ship's Book HMS *Invincible*: PRO Adm 136/8

Ship's Cover HMS *Invincible*: NMM

Ship's Log Books HMS *Invincible* (1909–13): PRO Adm 53/22244-22249

Ship's Log Books HMS *Invincible* (1914–16): PRO Adm 53/44888-44901

The Loss of HMS *Invincible*: PRO Adm 116/1535

Final Reports of model experiments. HMS *Invincible* (1906): PRO Adm 226/14

Ship's Log Books HMS *Indomitable* (1913–20): Adm 53/44828-44835

Ship's Log Books HMS *Inflexible* (1913–20): Adm 53/44388-44859

Confidential Navy Lists: PRO Adm 177/3-8

Naval Manoeuvres 1913: PRO Adm 116/1214

Progress in Naval Gunnery 1914–18: PRO Adm 186/238

The Battle Cruiser Force War Records (6 volumes): PRO Adm 137/2129–2134

The Grand Fleet Narrative (17 volumes): PRO Adm 137/414-430

The Action off The Falkland Islands: PRO Adm 137/304

The Action in The Heligoland Bight, 28 August 1914: PRO Adm 137/1943, Adm 137/551

Home Waters Telegrams: PRO Adm 137/50-233

Methods of firing used by HM Ships *Invincible* and *Inflexible* during the action off the Falklands: PRO Adm 1/8408/6

Cause of explosion in British warships when hit by heavy shell: PRO Adm 1/8463/176

Cabinet Office Historical Section official war histories: Correspondence and papers: Cab 45/269: Part I, Jutland correspondence; Part II, Seven lectures on Jutland by Captain J. H. Godfrey; Part V, Notes on Captain Dewar's lectures on Jutland

Grand Fleet Secret Packs, Volume 26, Miscellaneous Intelligence (Containing a translation of notes made during the Falklands' battle, of Midshipman Freiherr Grote, one of the survivors of *Gneisenau*): PRO Adm 137/1906

Director of Naval Construction, Admiralty 'Records of Warship Construction During the War, 1914–18': NL

Grand Fleet Gunnery and Torpedo Memoranda on Naval Actions 1914–18: NL

Commander W. G. Tennant. 'Jutland'. Seven Lectures: NMM

Commander John Creswell. 'The Battle of the Heligoland Bight'. Lecture: CCC

The Naval Staff Appreciation of Jutland, Roskill papers: CCC

Admiralty Typescript Translation of the German Official Account of Jutland: NL

Naval Staff War Histories, 1914–18:

  Passage of the British Expeditionary Force, August 1914: NL
  The Battle of Heligoland Bight: NL
  Home Waters – Part I. August 1914: NL
  Home Waters – Part II. September and October 1914: NL
  Home Waters – Part III. November 1914 – January 1915: PRO Adm 186/621
  Home Waters – Part IV. February – July 1915: PRO Adm 186/622
  Home Waters – Part V. July – October 1915: PRO Adm 186/623
  Home Waters – Part VI. October 1915 – May 1916. PRO Adm 186/624
  Home Waters – Part VII. June – November 1916: PRO Adm 86/628
  The Atlantic Ocean, 1914–15: PRO Adm 186/617
  Operations Leading up to the Battle of the Falkland Islands: PRO Adm 186/591
  Battles of Coronel and Falkland Islands: NL

Technical History Section, Admiralty. 'Storage and Handling of Explosives in Warships': NL

Beatty's Battle Cruiser Orders: Drax papers, CCC

The papers of Rear-Admiral The Hon. H. L. A. Hood: CCC

The papers of Vice-Admiral B. B. Schofield: IWM

The diary of Sub-Lieutenant R. R. Stewart: IWM

The diary of Midshipman Allan McEwan: IWM
The diary and letters of Midshipman Alexander Scrimgeour: IWM
The papers of Captain Arthur Dyce Duckworth: IWM
The diary of Assistant Paymaster Clement Woodland, RNR: NMM
The papers of Vice-Admiral T. N. James: IWM
The papers of Major W. F. Vernon: IWM
The diary of Ship's Corporal (HMS *Inflexible*) Marine Albert Lee: IWM
Author's correspondence with the late Rear-Admiral H. E. Dannreuther (1976)
Author's correspondence with Captain H. H. Dannreuther (1976)
Author's correspondence with Commander T. G. P. Crick (1976)
Author's correspondence and notes of conversations with Marine Gunner Bryan Gasson (the only living member of the six survivors of the sinking of *Invincible*) (1980)
Authors correspondence with Captain R. Ross Stewart, RN
Author's correspondence with Mrs Grace Duckworth (widow of Captain Arthur Dyce Duckworth, RN)
Author's correspondence with Mrs C. M. McEwan (widow of Lieutenant-Commander Allan McEwan).

PUBLISHED MATERIAL: OFFICIAL
Command and Parliamentary papers (HMSO)
Cmd. 1068 (1920). *Battle of Jutland. Official Dispatches.*
Cmd. 2870 (1927). *Reproduction of the Record of the Battle of Jutland*, by Captain J. E. T. Harper.
Corbett, Sir Julian S., and Newbolt, Sir Henry. *History of the Great War. Naval Operations*, Longmans, 1920–31, 5 vols.
Hansard Parliamentary Debates, 1905–14

PUBLISHED WORKS: GENERAL
Bayly, Admiral Sir Lewis. *Pull Together! The Memoirs of Admiral Sir Lewis Bayly.* Harrap, 1939
Bennett, Captain Geoffrey. *Coronel and the Falklands.* Batsford, 1962
Bingham, Commander the Hon. Barry. *Falklands, Jutland and the Bight.* Murray, 1919
Brassey's Naval Annual, 1905–25 editions
Campbell, N. J. M. *Battle Cruisers. Warship special No. 1.* Conway Maritime Press, 1978
Churchill, Sir Winston S. *The World Crisis 1911–1918.* Butterworth, 1923–31, 6 vols.

Fawcett, Lieutenant-Commander H. W., and Hooper, Lieutenant G. W. W. (eds.). *The Fighting at Jutland*. Macmillan, 1921

Fleming, H. M. Le. *Warships of World War One*. Ian Allan Ltd., 1961, 5 vols.

Frewen, Oswald. *Sailor's Soliloquy*. Hutchinson, 1961

Halpern, Paul G. *The Mediterranean Naval Situation 1908–1914*. Cambridge, Mass., Harvard University Press, 1970

Hase, Commander Georg Von. *Kiel and Jutland*. Skeffington, 1921

Hickling, Vice-Admiral Harold. *Sailor at Sea*. Kimber, 1965

Hirst, Paymaster Commander Lloyd. *Coronel and After*. Peter Davies, 1934

Hough, Richard. *The Pursuit of Admiral Von Spee: a study in Loneliness and Bravery*. Allen and Unwin, 1969

Hough, Richard. *First Sea Lord: an Authorised Biography of Admiral Lord Fisher*. Allen and Unwin, 1969

Jellicoe, Admiral of the Fleet, Earl. *The Grand Fleet, 1914–1916*. Cassell, 1919

Kemp, Lieutenant-Commander P. K. *The Papers Of Admiral Sir John Fisher*. Navy Records Society, 1960–64, 2 vols.

Kerr, Admiral Mark. *Land, Sea and Air*. Longmans, 1927

Kerr, Admiral Mark. *The Navy in My Time*. Rich and Cowan, 1933

Lumby, E. W. R. (ed.). *Papers Relating to Naval Policy and Operations in the Mediterranean, 1911–1915*. Navy Records Society, 1970

Marder, Arthur J. *From the Dreadnought to Scapa Flow*. Oxford University Press, 1961–70, 5 vols.

Marder, Arthur J. *British Naval Policy, 1880–1905: the Anatomy of British Sea Power*. Putnam, 1941

Patterson, A. Temple (ed.). *The Jellicoe Papers*. Navy Records Society, 1966–68, 2 vols.

Pochhammer, Captain Hans. *Before Jutland: Admiral Von Spee's last Voyage*. Jarrolds, 1931

Pollard, Sidney, and Robertson, Paul. *The British Ship Building Industry 1870–1914*. Cambridge, Mass., Harvard Studies in Business History, 1979

Roberts, John A. *Warship Monographs: Invincible Class*. Conway Maritime Press, 1972

Roskill, Captain Stephen, R.N. *Admiral of The Fleet Earl Beatty. The Last Naval Hero*. Collins, 1980

Young, Filson. *With the Battle Cruisers*. Cassell, 1921

NEWSPAPERS AND PERIODICALS

The Times (1907–16)

The Newcastle Weekly Chronicle (1907)

Blackwood's Magazine (1916): four articles by Paymaster Gordon Franklyn

The London Magazine (1916) article by Able Seaman E. Dandridge entitled 'The Price of Victory'.

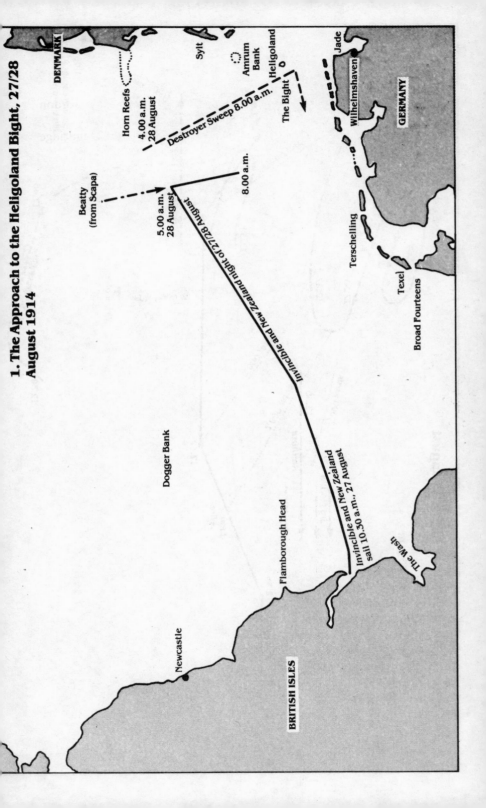

1. The Approach to the Heligoland Bight, 27/28 August 1914

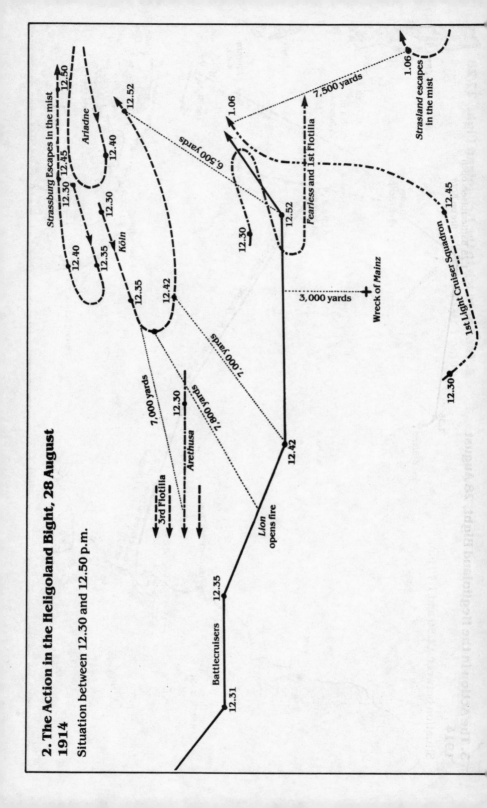

2. The Action in the Heligoland Bight, 28 August 1914

Situation between 12.30 and 12.50 p.m.

Strassburg Escapes in the mist

12.50
12.45
12.30
Ariadne
12.40

12.30
12.40
12.35
Köln
12.30

12.52
12.35
12.42

6,500 yards

1.06
1.06
Strasland escapes in the mist
7,500 yards
Fearless and 1st Flotilla

12.52
12.30

3,000 yards
Wreck of Mainz

7,000 yards
7,000 yards
7,800 yards

3rd Flotilla
12.30
Arethusa

12.42
Lion opens fire

12.35
Battlecruisers

12.31

1st Light Cruiser Squadron
12.45
12.30

3. The Action in the Heglioland Bight, 28 August 1914

Situation between 12.56 and 1.40 p.m.

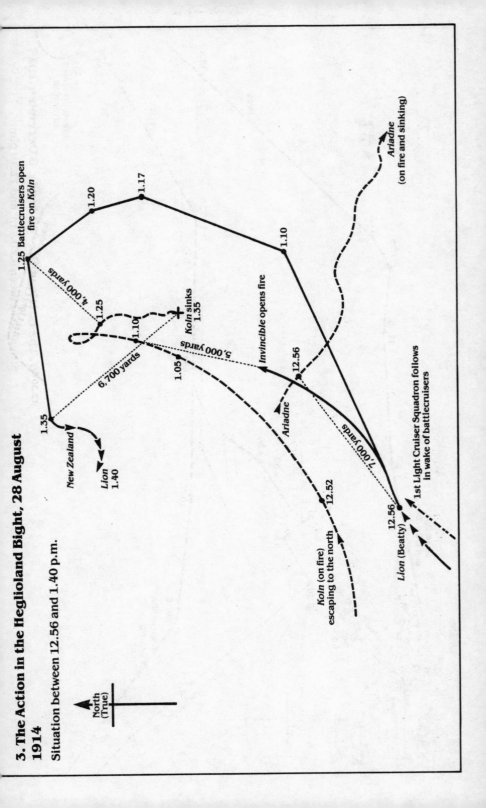

North (True)

1.25 Battlecruisers open fire on *Köln*

1.20

1.17

1.25

4,000 yards

1.25

1.10

New Zealand

1.35

Lion 1.40

6,700 yards

Köln sinks 1.55

5,000 yards

1.05

Invincible opens fire

1.10

Ariadne

12.56

Ariadne (on fire and sinking)

7,000 yards

1st Light Cruiser Squadron follows in wake of battlecruisers

12.52

Köln (on fire) escaping to the north

12.56

Lion (Beatty)

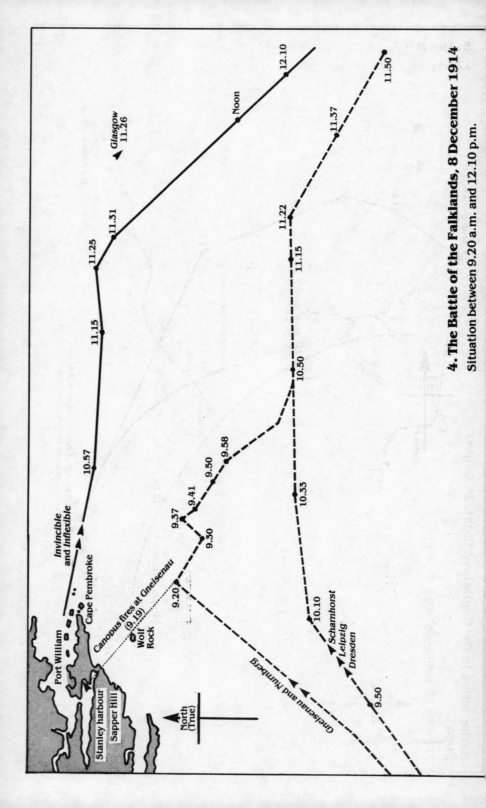

4. The Battle of the Falklands, 8 December 1914
Situation between 9.20 a.m. and 12.10 p.m.

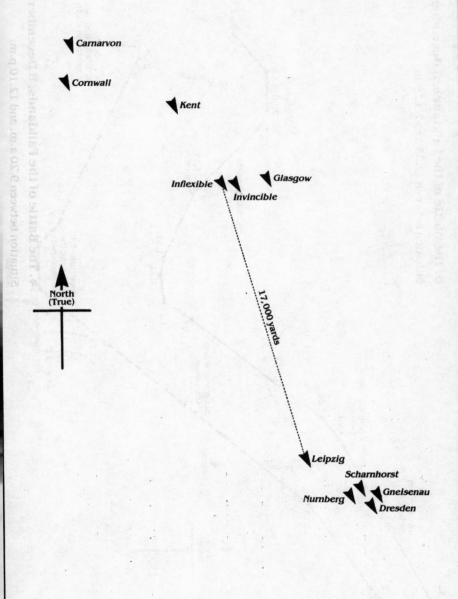

5. The Battle of the Falklands, 8 December 1914

12.55 p.m. – *Inflexible* opens fire

Carnarvon

Cornwall

Kent

Inflexible

Invincible

Glasgow

North
(True)

17,000 yards

Leipzig

Scharnhorst

Nurnberg

Gneisenau

Dresden

0   yards   10,000

6. The Battle of the Falklands, 8 December 1914
Situation between 12.33 and 2.12 p.m.

7. The Battle of the Falklands, 8 December 1914

Situation between 2.10 and 6.10 p.m.

2.26

Invincible and
Inflexible

2.36

2.43

2.47
2.48 *Invincible* opens fire

North
(true)

Var 9° 35′ E

Gneisenau and
Scharnhorst

2.35

2.48

15,000 yards

2.54
2.56   3.00   3.03

3.25   3.20

3.15
3.10

3.30

3.37

11,000 yards

3.46

3.42   3.12

3.52

3.03

3.55

3.57

14,000 yards

3.27
3.37   3.32

4.01

3.50

4.24   4.30
4.06   4.34

4.03

4.52

Inflexible's track
in dotted line

Invincible
5.07

4.20   4.17
5.00
Scharnhorst
sinks

4.17

5.11
Inflexible

4.23

5.18

5.48

4.25
4.29

5.12

5.40

4.35

4.41

5.32

5.09

5.15

5.57   6.10
6.04

5.23

5.55

Gneisenau
sinks
6.02

5.30

5.47
5.42

5.35

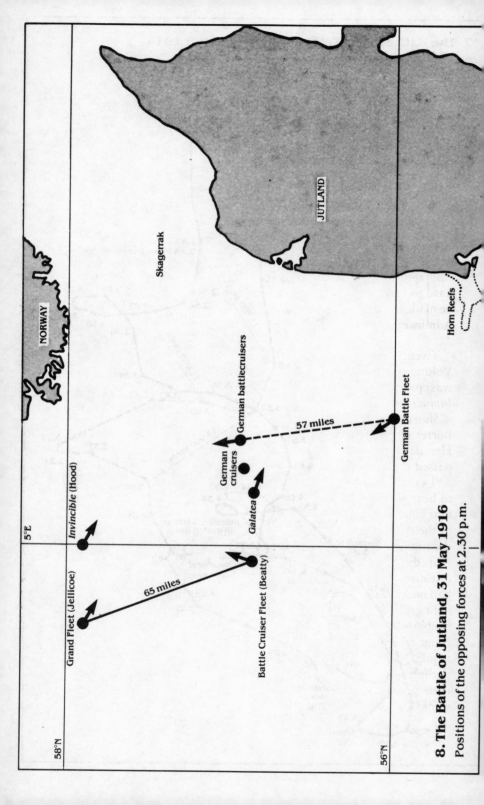

8. The Battle of Jutland, 31 May 1916
Positions of the opposing forces at 2.30 p.m.

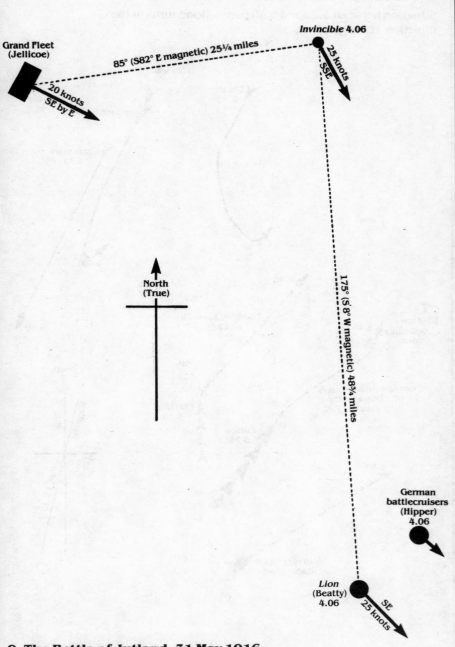

9. The Battle of Jutland, 31 May 1916

Situation at 4.06 p.m., showing the relative positions of
Beatty and Jellicoe from *Invincible* when Hood changed course
to SSE to support the Battle Cruiser Fleet

10. The Battle of Jutland, 31 May 1916

Situation between 5.20 and 5.40 p.m. — Hood turns in the direction of the gun flashes.

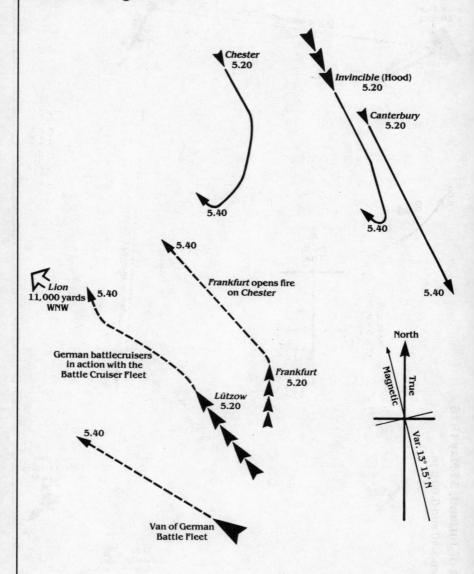

Chester
5.20

Invincible (Hood)
5.20

Canterbury
5.20

5.40

5.40

5.40

5.40

Frankfurt opens fire on *Chester*

Lion
11,000 yards
WNW

5.40

German battlecruisers
in action with the
Battle Cruiser Fleet

Frankfurt
5.20

Lützow
5.20

5.40

North

Magnetic

True

Var. 13° 15′ N

Van of German
Battle Fleet

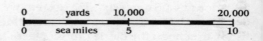

0	yards	10,000	20,000
0	sea miles	5	10

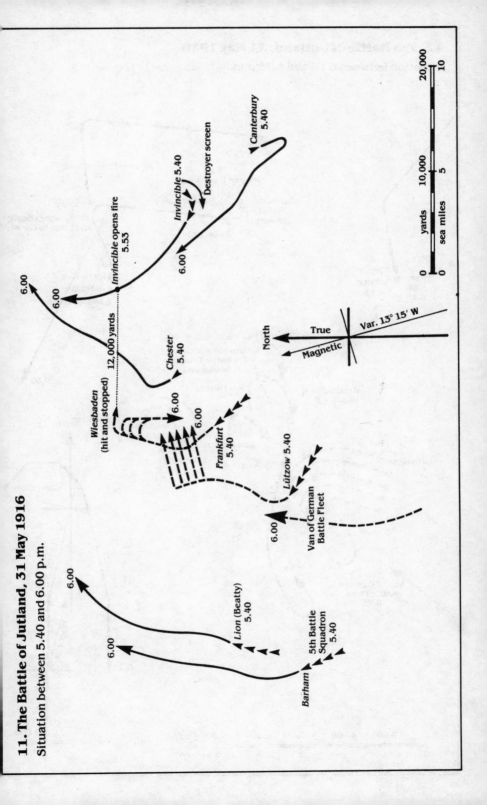

11. The Battle of Jutland, 31 May 1916
Situation between 5.40 and 6.00 p.m.

Canterbury 5.40

Destroyer screen

Invincible 5.40

Invincible opens fire 5.53

6.00

6.00

Chester 5.40

12,000 yards

Wiesbaden (hit and stopped)

6.00

6.00

Frankfurt 5.40

Lützow 5.40

6.00

Van of German Battle Fleet

North

True

Magnetic

Var. 13° 15' W

6.00

6.00

Lion (Beatty) 5.40

Barham 5.40

5th Battle Squadron 5.40

yards   0   10,000   20,000

sea miles 0   5   10

12. The Battle of Jutland, 31 May 1916

Situation between 6.00 and 6.15 p.m.

6.15

German torpedoes

Invincible
(helm
jammed)

Indomitable

Chester

Hood sights Beatty
and turns to the west

Inflexible

Invincible

Inflexible

Indomitable

Lion
6.15

Warrior
Defence
6.15

(Engaging Wiesbaden)

12th half Flotilla

Torpedo attack on
3rd Battle Cruiser
Squadron

9th Flotilla

Weisbaden
(disabled)

Shark
Acasta
Christopher —attacking
Ophelia

2nd Flotilla

Lützow

Frankfurt

6.15

6.15

Canterbury

North

Van of German
Battle Fleet
6.15

6.15

Magnetic

True

Var. 13° 15' W

0	2,000	4,000	6,000	8,000	10,000 yards
0	1	2	3	4	5 sea miles

13. The Battle of Jutland, 31 May 1916

Situation between 6.15 and 6.26 p.m., showing *Invincible* in the van of the fleet.

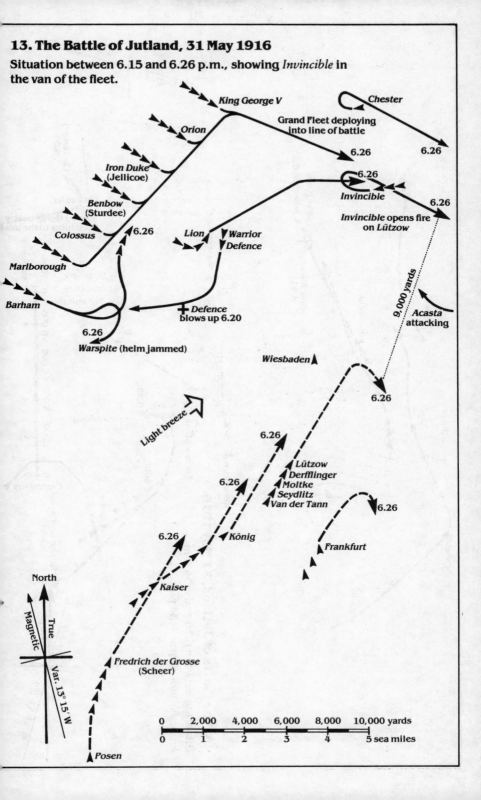

King George V

Chester

Orion

Grand Fleet deploying
into line of battle

6.26   6.26

Iron Duke
(Jellicoe)

6.26

Invincible   6.26

Invincible opens fire
on *Lützow*

Benbow
(Sturdee)

Colossus   6.26   Lion   Warrior
                                                         Defence

Marlborough

Barham

9,000 yards

Acasta
attacking

Defence
blows up 6.20

6.26

6.26

Warspite (helm jammed)

Wiesbaden

6.26

Light breeze

6.26

Lützow
Derfflinger
Moltke
Seydlitz
Van der Tann

6.26

6.26

König   6.26

Frankfurt

6.26

Kaiser

North

Magnetic True

Var. 13° 15' W

Fredrich der Grosse
(Scheer)

Posen

0	2,000	4,000	6,000	8,000	10,000 yards
0	1	2	3	4	5 sea miles

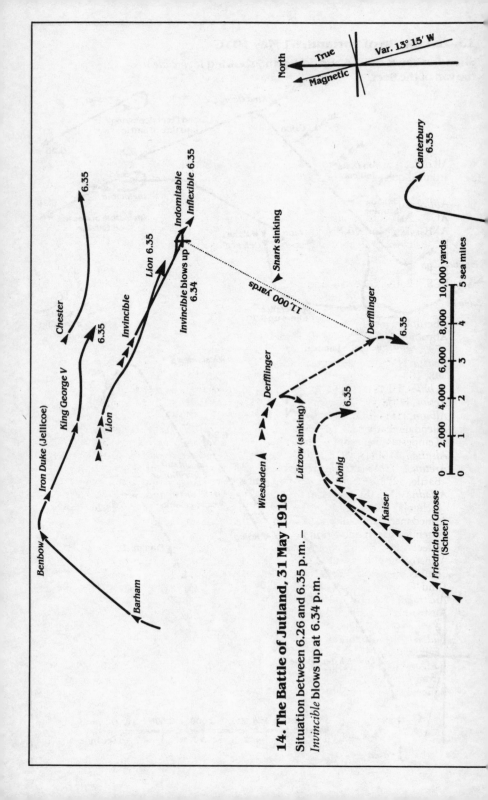

Var. 13° 15' W

North
True
Magnetic

6.35

Canterbury
6.35

Snark sinking

Indomitable
Inflexible 6.35

Lion 6.35

Invincible blows up
6.34

11,000 yards

6.35

Chester

King George V

Invincible

Derfflinger

Derfflinger

Lion

Wiesbaden

Derfflinger

Lützow (sinking)

6.35

Benbow

Iron Duke (Jellicoe)

König

Kaiser

Barham

Friedrich der Grosse
(Scheer)

0   2,000   4,000   6,000   8,000   10,000 yards
0   1   2   3   4   5 sea miles

14. The Battle of Jutland, 31 May 1916

Situation between 6.26 and 6.35 p.m. —
Invincible blows up at 6.34 p.m.

Index

All officers and titled people are indexed under the highest rank and title attained during the period this book covers.

Abbreviations:

AC	Armoured cruiser	BS	Battle Squadron
AMC	Armed merchant cruiser	C	Cruiser
B	Dreadnought battleship	CS	Cruiser Squadron
BC	Battlecruiser	LC	Light cruiser
BCF	Battlecruiser Fleet	LCS	Light Cruiser Squadron
BCS	Battlecruiser Squadron	PD	Predreadnought battleship

153

154